The Trust Equation

Successful Financial Advisors Speak Out on

Integrity, Client Relationships

the Wealth Management Process

Steven Drozdeck • Lyn Fisher

Publisher

Financial Forum Publishing

(435) 750-0062

Printer:

Monroe Litho

(585) 454-3290

Table of Contents

Trust does not happen immediately or accidentally. It is usually based on certain objective and subjective "proofs" that, cumulatively, bring us to the point or threshold of saying that a person is trustworthy or reliable. Similarly, with friendship or love there is a point where someone moves from an acquaintance to the next level based upon such factors as mutual interests, being there, listening and understanding, etc.

For children, trust is often easy. As soon as they share a piece of candy, play together on the playground, walk together in line, or smile at one another, children become friends. Adults are more hesitant. We know we can't take everything at face value – we have to check certain things out. We want to judge how we react to someone and how they react to us. We learn to trust someone who really understands our needs and tries to help whenever possible. That someone should complement our abilities, reduce our weaknesses, and enhance our strengths. And, that person should fit well in other aspects of our lives.

All of these things, plus many others, are part of a mental equation that allows us to judge a person. The same is true in the financial services industry and for this book. We've helped quantify some of the elements of trust by examining the important factors. With the help of 19 high-level advisors, we explored concepts such as business practices, the need for integrity, and educational requirements to provide a higher level of professionalism. These advisors are industry leaders and are (or should be) the model for discerning clients. Regardless of their years in the business, they all share common traits; a commitment to excellence, a desire to help their clients fulfill their goals, and a high level of integrity. Most importantly, they really care about their clients. Each chapter begins with a statement defining integrity from each of these professionals. Take time to read them, and you'll discover the depth of their commitment to their clients.

As a client, you can do a number of things to help ensure that the advisor you pick to provide a high-level, comprehensive financial plan and/or manage some or all of your money is the right person for you. These things include: knowing what personal and financial objectives you wish to achieve; getting referrals from other trusted professionals; asking astute questions and listening to the answers carefully; educating yourself on investment matters; maintaining consistency in your approach; and allowing the advisor the time needed to produce results.

Each chapter in this book discusses a different piece of the trust equation and allows you to more fully understand the role of an advisor and what your current advisor is—or is not—doing for you. You also will learn how to be a better client. *The Trust Equation* is about more than merely trust and integrity. It is about the elements and people who define these two essential qualities.

Acknowledgements

*W*riting a book is never a one-person effort, and The Trust Equation *is no exception. It would never have been completed without the help and support of the following people.*

Special thanks to:

Sydney LeBlanc who provided on-going support to bring this project to fruition. Along with interviewing some of the advisors, she advised, contributed and encouraged us throughout.

Gina Lauer for her meticulous editing and proof-reading. She's a great friend and a true pro.

Our professional staff: Cami Miller, Alison Hobbs, Channary Leng, and Rebecca Kirby.

Stephen Winks for his contributions and Jeff Prekopa for his technical assistance.

And a sincere thank you to the 19 financial advisors who took time out of their busy schedules to participate in this project. They provided an abundance of insight into the attributes required for an advisor to be truly great. They are sterling examples that integrity and trust are alive and thriving!

Steven Drozdeck

Lyn Fisher

A tidal wave of change is occurring in the financial services industry. Financial institutions, such as banks, brokerage firms, and insurance companies, that have dominated the scene for the past 100 years have undergone massive internal changes. New business structures, computerization, worldwide competition, and changing consumer needs are a few of the reasons for these major changes.

The information revolution and the development of powerful desktop computers allowed some pioneers to think outside the box and understand the dynamics of the financial markets in new ways. Modern Portfolio Theory (MPT) is one example. The revolutionary way the Chicago Board of Options Exchange (CBOE) allowed options to be traded caused another major shift in how the markets could be approached. These are merely two examples of new thoughts and processes that changed the potential and scope of the worldwide financial marketplace. Today, the institutions still exist, but the products and services they provide now overlap tremendously. Brokerage firms offer banking and insurance products, insurance agents offer mutual funds, and bankers offer insurance products and securities. Even more significant is the advent of the "independent (financial) advisor," whose services are the subject of this book. Taking advantage of the financial evolution and revolution, these new-breed advisors have a wealth of capabilities to allow them to more effectively manage your money. These professionals follow a new business model that offers a more focused approach to selling financial products and services.

This book covers three continuums within the financial services industry that are important to you, the investor. These three continuums are advice, education (and experience), and compensation.

Advice Continuum: Many of you have probably received telephone calls from high-energy, persuasive promoters offering the latest "hot stock" that's going to double in the next few months. They *only* want "a commitment of a few thousand shares so you can get your feet wet." They make sales pitches without knowing anything about you except that you may have invested in the market before. Such people represent the extreme low-end of the advice continuum. While this approach may be okay for certain well-heeled, highly speculative sophisticated investors, most people should avoid those "opportunities of a lifetime." This type of advisor usually makes no attempt to determine suitability, as required by the New York Stock Exchange, and is only interested in making the sale. As former First Lady Barbara Bush said, "Just say no!"

Moving up the advice continuum: While the vast majority of advisors offer a large array of financial products and services made available through their companies, many only ask you minimal information about your goals and objectives before making a recommendation. In general, the less the advisor knows about you, the more of a cookie-cutter solution you will receive.

At the top of the advice continuum: These advisors will ask a more comprehensive set of questions, thereby gaining a better and broader understanding of your needs and objectives. Therefore, these advisors usually recommend more customized solutions. The highest-level advisors won't make any recommendations until they have a thorough understanding of your financial needs and status. Their financial solutions are often the best crafted and most precisely tailored to your specific needs. They are members of various industry associations and continually refresh and upgrade their knowledge base. Experience also is an important consideration in selecting an adviser. Ask yourself the question, "Do you want an advisor with a lot of experience or one who will be using *you* to gain experience for the future?" Of course, knowledge and experience only count if they are the *right kinds* of knowledge and experience. This is the *education continuum.*

Compensation continuum: How does a financial advisor get paid? If pay is commission-based, the advisor has a vested interest in selling you financial products and services. Fee-only advisors, on the other hand, are paid for the advice rendered and do not receive additional compensation from you or any other party.

It is important to understand that being compensated by commissions is not necessarily bad. In fact, it is appropriate in some instances. Most financial advisors who receive commissions are good, caring and knowledgeable people, interested in doing the right thing for you because that is how they maintain a long-term relationship with you and other clients and get referral business.

As in any industry, abuses can occur. Financial advisors, stockbrokers and insurance agents, can all get a bad name because of the poor ethics and business practices of a small group. These abuses, however, lead to government regulation, as well as new approaches and standards. As a result, those employed in the financial services industry find new ways to step out of the box, change the paradigms, and offer their services. The advisors featured in this book have done just that. They have made sure that they always sit on the same side of the table as their clients.

In the pages ahead you will gain an insight into how to work with these 19 advisors with different backgrounds, clientele, and experience. We asked them to respond to questions that you, as a client, would have. You'll find what to look for in an advisor, what to reasonably expect, what an advisor expects from you, and learn from the mistakes of other clients. If you are a financial advisor yourself, you'll discover industry best practices from some very accomplished individuals that will help you advise your own clients more effectively.

BROMELKAMP ON INTEGRITY

"A person is not given *integrity*. It results from the relentless pursuit of honesty at all times."

David J. Bromelkamp, CIMA
Senior Consulting Group
RBC Dain Rauscher

CHAPTER 1

Solving the Trust Dilemma

M any financial advisors, including those interviewed for this book, first began working with retail clients, or individuals and small businesses, rather
than with institutional clients looking for assistance with
pension and profit-sharing plans. No matter what type of
firm these retail advisors might work for — bank, brokerage house, or insurance company; international, national, regional, or local—they usually sell products and
services for a commission. They often give excellent financial advice, but their pay is dependant on selling products, such as mutual funds, securities, bonds and insurance.
They earn a commission when they sell these products, and
don't get paid outright for their knowledge or abilities.

Many advisors, however, would prefer to bring their
knowledge and experience to the table, offering financial
advice that is in the best interests of a client and not influenced by commissions generated when selling their
firm's proprietary products and services.[1]

To be successful, traditional, commission-based advisors must be good salespeople, earning the trust of clients who will feel comfortable following the advisor's
recommendations. Many advisors transition from a sales-
oriented business to concentrate on what they do best –

providing high-level, comprehensive advice. They interview clients and offer strategies that allow clients to attain their financial goals instead of persuading those clients to buy or sell something. Just like doctors, lawyers, CPAs and other professionals, they are hired to provide expert counsel, not to sell products. They receive professional fees for their knowledge, specialized skills, and experience.

Many advisors don't want to "play" the stock market with all of its vagaries and ups and downs. They don't have the time to monitor the market's day-to-day fluctuations. Advisors would rather evaluate and monitor the performance of professional money managers[2].

Rather than helping clients achieve a limited number of financial goals, these advisors prefer to look at a client's overall picture and develop a comprehensive financial plan. Many advisors have the talent and disposition to be the maestro that directs the entire orchestra of financial service providers.

These special advisors have developed specialized business approaches that serve the needs of a select clientele. Think of them as high-level financial advisors or investment management consultants, even though they are referred to as "financial advisors" throughout this book.

Jack Krapf, senior vice president, Aldridge, Johnson & Krapf Wealth Management Group of Wachovia Securities (Macon, GA), entered the investment business at age 25 in 1985. He had studied accounting and finance at the Citadel and practiced public accounting for two and one-half years. He recounts, "As a young broker, I started out purely 100 percent transaction [commission based]. After the crash of 1987, I realized that security selection was not my [area of] expertise." He made a decision to become an institutional investment consultant, and it took him almost five years to fully transition his business to fee-based.

New Business Model

David J. Bromelkamp, senior vice president of RBC Dain Rauscher (Minneapolis, MN), was featured in the December 2002 issue of *Twin Cities Business Monthly*. The article states, "Starting in the brokerage business in 1988, Bromelkamp did business the old-fashioned way. That is, he made cold calls, generally selling the stock or bond of the month. His job was to make transactions, his reward was commissions.

But in 1995, he began his conversion to a new business model. Recast as a financial consultant, he helps clients choose professional money managers. Now he works for fees, not commissions. The process imposes an investment strategy and discipline on his clients, elements that are often missing from the traditional stock brokerage model, he says.

Bromelkamp is not alone in this, of course. Firms like Merrill Lynch, for example, have been pushing their brokers to act less like brokers and more like asset gathers and money managers. But Bromelkamp draws the distinctions with a sharp edge as he maps out the old and new world orders for colleagues at Daine Rauscher's downtown Minneapolis office, and for outside audiences. As his lists show, he can't resist tweaking the old while he sells the new."

Dave Bromelkamp's World of Financial Services	
Old World Order	*New World Order*
Broker	Consultant
Commissions	Fees
Transactions	Advice
Give away advice	Give away trades
Charge for trades	Charge for advice
Sales culture	Professionalism
Sales skills	Professional credentials
Many accounts	Few relationships
Transaction-based	Process-oriented
Individual	Team
Generalists	Specialists
Security selection	Modern portfolio theory
Unrelated transactions	Comprehensive solution
Hidden Costs	Transparency
Stock pickers	Wealth managers

The Transition to Fee-Base Planning

Donald R. Parker, CFA®, AVA, founder of Gryphon Valuation Consultants (Las Vegas, NV), recounts, "It was sometime in 1984 or 85. My responsibility, besides managing the portfolios, was marketing the products to individual brokers in the larger wire houses[3]. Anybody who didn't already have a book [clients] just wasn't interested because they had to create current income via commissions. But those who were more seasoned, and had substantial books, were already transitioning their business to managed accounts… they didn't have to [or want to] wake up and sell somebody something every day."

Why don't more advisors provide fee-based financial plans? The switch can be expensive. As Jeffrey B. Thomas, Raymond James Financial Services Inc. (Dallas, TX), explains: "I became a full-time, fee-based advisor in 1966, after landing a very large 401(k) account which provided sufficient capital to carry me through the transition. I immediately went fee-based at that time. Now, including fees from 401(k) plans, I'm substantially fee based."

Traditional brokers who switch to a fee-based business must give up a lot of commission income and often lose numerous clients who wouldn't benefit from this new type of business structure, because either their accounts are too small or their investment objectives cannot be met by an outside money manager. It often takes two to four years to make the transition, during which time the loss of clients and income stream can be quite significant. Advisors must be willing to pay the price – in terms of financial costs and educational requirements – to make the shift. The change takes commitment and dedication.

So why do some advisors make the change? Frederick "Fred" J. Dawson, founding partner and vice president of Bassett, Brosius & Dawson, Inc. (Wilmington, DE), recounts the turning point in his career. Dawson, who started out in the insurance industry, went to visit a prospect who was an executive at a major manufacturing firm. Immediately he realized the prospect knew more than he did and was at a higher sophistication level. Fred shares, "I wasn't there a half-hour before he 'bloodied my nose,' so to speak. I didn't understand what he was talking about. I couldn't answer any of his questions or refute many of his statements. I didn't have any education that would help me in this situation. At that point I made the determination that, because of this one guy, I was going to get an education. I went on to get my Chartered Financial Consultant (ChFC) and Chartered Life Underwriter (CLU) designations[4]. I started attending industry conferences. The more I learned the more I realized I wanted to do more for my clients than just offer insurance products. It was at that point I began transitioning from an insurance agent to becoming a comprehensive wealth manager. I've never had any regrets."

Doing What's Right for the Client

Dawson is not alone in his aspiration for a high level of professional education. He and others in this book wanted to expand their knowledge and become true experts in their fields.

A good example is Martim DeArantes-Oliveira, a principal of H&S Financial Advisors (Menlo Park, CA), who manages a wealth management practice within an accounting firm. DeArantes-Oliveira mentions how many accountants are getting into the investment advice business because they are "shocked by what they see some financial advisors doing and decided it wasn't in the best interest of their clients." While with a major brokerage firm, he felt "really torn between doing the right thing or doing what the client wanted. It isn't just about industry salespeople getting the client to buy things. A lot of it was driven by clients. There was this whole mentality that the markets have changed and would keep going up.

"In the brokerage industry model, if you were a broker in 1998-99, it was very difficult to live off your commissions and maintain a more conservative investment strategy. Obviously, as a broker you have total discretion as to the type of clients you have, but it would have been very difficult in that model and compensation structure to 'stick to your guns.'

Brent E. Bentrim, managing principal of Carolopolis Family Wealth Management, Inc. tells the following story:

"I began my career at a large wire house that espoused advice and planning in its marketing materials while, at the same time, lobbying the SEC to be exempt from the 1940 Investment Advisors Act because 'advice was only ancillary to its core business of transacting.' I was bored trying to be something I really had no skill for – being a salesman. I hated trying to convince clients that at the age of 26, I had control over the market. I was tired of financial jargon and not having the opportunity to interact with my clients.

I think the final straw was drawn in the fall of 2000 when a sales manager thought 'I had too much cash in client accounts,' and suggested I follow suit of another broker who was placing all of his clients in a technology Unit Investment Trusts because they were down 15 percent and 'certainly could not go lower.' Needless to say, I did not follow the advice of the sales manager. It was ironic, however, that the other broker, while losing almost 80 percent of the client's investment, received praise and recognition for selling such high-commissioned products which generated tremendous revenue for the firm. I then realized that it was up to me to create a better alternative. I went independent, founded my own Registered Investment Advisory (RIA), and only solicited clients that I enjoyed and for whom I could truly add value."

"I was lucky enough to be relatively successful in the area that I worked and, with the type of clients I had, to be able to stick to my guns. But in the wire house mentality, I would say it was virtually impossible. That's why a lot of wire house brokers have left to begin new careers. They just didn't feel right always doing what the clients want them to."

A Fragmented Market

Ira G. Rapaport, vice president of RINET Company, LLC (Boston, MA), was one of the advisors who realized that the demand for high-level, comprehensive advice wasn't being met in today's competitive financial services industry. "The market is extremely fragmented," he says, "People are looking for sophisticated advice that is personally customized and objective. They are looking to have a long-term, trusting relationship with an advisor who will put together a strategy that is consistent with their goals and objectives."

Adam Westphalen, chief investment officer and co-founder of Vista Financial Strategies, LLC (Stratford, CT), sums it up by saying, "It's nice being able to work with a client and have a spouse say, 'We're really grateful that you're working with us. I feel really secure.' That's what makes it worthwhile."

---

1. Some firms pay higher commissions if the advisor sells a proprietary product or service. Additionally, some firms put pressure on their salespeople to promote them because there is greater revenue for the firm. This practice is discouraged by industry regulators, yet it is still a common practice. Products, such as mutual funds, created by the firm, generate greater commissions than a similar mutual fund not owned by the brokerage firm.

2. A professional portfolio manager hired to manage client accounts. Each has a particular investment approach that they are expected to adhere to.

3. The term dates back to the time when only the largest organizations had access to high-speed communications. It is still used to refer to the biggest brokerage houses.

4. A description of many industry designations is provided in Chapter 17.

KRAPF ON INTEGRITY

"As a Citadel graduate, it is my belief that in order to live a godly life it is very important to have honor and *integrity* in everything I do as a man. To develop long-term relationships with clients is a matter of clients perceiving an individual's honesty and trustworthiness. Caring about doing the right things for our clients, and making sure that whatever we do as consultants is what we believe is absolutely the right things to do. Even if mistakes are made, if you care and try to fix the problems, your clients will understand. Continually educating yourself, providing the best advice you can, and being honest and forthright is not only how we should live our lives but the way we should conduct business."

Jack R. Krapf, CIMA
Aldridge, Johnson & Krapf of
Wachovia Securities

CHAPTER 2

PROCESS
- A course or method of operations in the production of something.
- A forward movement or continuous development.
- To prepare by a special method.

Importance of a Process

One of the major distinctions between high-level financial advisors and traditional advisors is their strict adherence to specific disciplines and processes. In other words, they follow systematic, proven methods to chart the right financial course for each client.

Any time you take a trip, you know there are a number of roads that will allow you to reach your destination. However, some routes are more direct and efficient than others. Similarly, in choosing a financial destination, some routes are more direct and provide more consistent results. If you have an important goal to achieve, why take a chance on getting random results – perhaps missing your goal completely? Instead, you can significantly boost your probability of financial success by employing an advisor with a proven track record of helping others reach similar goals.

Each of the high-level advisors interviewed for this book learned numerous investment disciplines that have proven effective over the years. These strategies are the same ones used by the sophisticated money managers and investors in the world. Financial advisors learn specific investment disciplines and then enhance their knowledge through experience and continuing education.

Using Qualified Professionals to Achieve Superior Results

Consider this analogy: If you or a loved one needs a complex surgery, you would seek out a surgeon with a high level of training, a successful history of performing similar operations, and substantial knowledge of the most recent medical advances. You would ask other professionals for referrals, check on the surgeon's reputation, and simultaneously learn all you can about the medical condition.

You would also expect the surgeon, and his/her entire staff, to systematically follow an established process or procedure. This process would probably start with a thorough examination, taking into account your overall physical condition. Next, your condition and surgery would be explained to you, and all of your questions answered. If you agreed to the operation, additional examinations might occur. On the day of the operation, surgery team members would be present to perform their various functions. After the procedure, you would be checked and monitored. Then, by following the doctor's recommended regimen for recovery, and with periodic checkups, you would find yourself in good health again.

The same holds true for all the important financial advisors in your life. These advisors might include an accountant, attorney, trust specialist, etc. It's important to surround yourself with the best team you can draw upon— professionals who will help you maintain your maximum financial health.

You want to work with a high-level financial advisor who has years of experience, a proven discipline , and has continually upgraded his/her knowledge. The advisor should have an excellent reputation, proven by on-going records of success and high levels of service. This person should work with well-trained and highly educated associates, whose expertise also can be drawn upon.

In the surgery analogy, you'll remember that responsibilities were shared by the patient and the medical team. The same is true in the financial world. You, the investor, must carry certain responsibilities, such as asking for and checking references, and asking relevant questions of both the advisors and their references. In addition, you must understand the process, go for periodic follow-up evaluations, and, of course, keep in contact with the advisor.

A Dual Responsibility

Throughout this book, your responsibilities as an investor, those of the advisor, and methods to evaluate the performance of the advisor, your portfolio, and your relationship, will be discussed. To a limited extent, you are being evaluated, too. That's because throughout the entire process your advisors should constantly assess all components of your financial plan, including you. Advisors want their clients to communicate with them, to provide them with any changes or updates in their financial condition, or any change of objectives. This information may lead to some changes in your financial plan and/or portfolios. If you – or any other client — insist on a course of action that is contrary to your best interests and against the advisor's business philosophy, the advisor may decline to work with you in the future.

The next 10 chapters discuss a process that allows you to select, monitor and evaluate your advisor. You will learn what an advisor does for you and receive an excellent overview into the practices of high-level financial advisors.

It is important to realize that there is a lot of overlap, or interdependence of processes with many of the activities occurring simultaneously. The process is similar to the movements of gears within a watch (non-digital, that is). If one part of the mechanism breaks down, the watch does not fulfill its function of keeping accurate time.

IMPORTANCE OF PROCESS

On a scale of 1 (lowest) to 10 (highest), each advisor interviewed for this book was asked to rate the importance of having a process for preparing a financial plan. The lowest rating given by an advisor was 10, with one rating at 12 and another at 25! Obviously, all these advisors think a process is vital, as do various licensing and certification agencies/associations throughout the world. A process helps ensure consistent results. It makes sure that nothing slips between the cracks. It helps ensure ongoing excellence. And, most importantly, the process is constantly being refined.

Thomas Curran, managing director, Curran Investment Management of Wachovia Securities (Albany, NY), suggests that a good process must be firmly entrenched and take the broadest objectives, such as long-term growth and income, and feed it into an investment solution. He explains, "In our business we have too many solutions for each problem and [can] eventually lose track of the whole management process."

Unfortunately, some advisors focus on individual products and services offered by their firm and often fail to realize the many ways an investment solution can be crafted. As a result, clients get parts of a solution. Like the watch, all the pieces may there, but it takes a skilled watchmaker to put them together into a working timepiece. High-level advisors are like watchmakers. If they have a defined, proven process, a client will receive a solution that leaves very little, if anything, to chance.

The PROCESS

Prepare

Research/Review

Objectives

Communicate

Execute/Evaluate

Systems

Synchronize

Here is another way to define the word "process" to give you a set of procedures that you can use to help attain investment success.

The next two chapters explain how both you and the advisor must prepare for a financial meeting. As an investor, you must get referrals, define your objectives, perform due diligence, etc. Advisors prepare by increasing their knowledge and by creating strategic alliances with other professionals. While they are reviewing your objectives with you, discussing reasonable expectations, and deciding if you are a viable client, you should be evaluating them and deciding if you feel comfortable with them and their business approach. Again, it's like a watch: Many things are happening simultaneously.

So, what constitutes expert financial advice? Here are some of the factors a financial advisor must consider when working with a client:

1. Determine precisely what a client's desired outcomes or objectives are.

2. Evaluate all of a client's finances – insurances, real estate holdings, financial investments and private holdings – in light of the

client's objectives and the big picture.

3. Consider the tax and legal consequences of each individual item or group of items held by the individual or within different legal entities/structures. Alternative approaches should also be considered.

4. Employ appropriate technologies.

5. "Know what you don't know" and be willing to bring in additional outside expert advice to assist in attaining client objectives. That is, use a team approach when appropriate.

6. Orchestrate all the expert knowledge and efforts to produce effective results.

7. Develop precise, written plans to accomplish macro and tactical goals.

8. Develop contingency plans.

9. Monitor approaches employed against changing market conditions.

10. Adapt plans when necessary.

11. Ensure the goals will be accomplished, even without your direct help.

12. Make sure a client understands the essence of your plans.

People, Process, Performance and Philosophy

David Bromelkamp says the process is a key element of his "4-Ps" equation. When asked, "How does an investor find a good financial advisor?" Bromelkamp responds by suggesting they select one in the same way that a financial professional selects professional money managers. He continues, "The research analysts like to talk about the 4 Ps: people, process, performance, philosophy— We also recommend that you ask a prospective financial advisor the following questions:

1) For individual investors: Are you a Certified Financial Planner (CFP®)? Are you a member of the Financial Planning Association? What is your investment process? What is your investment philosophy?

2) For fiduciary investors: Are you a Certified Investment Man-

agement Analyst (CIMA)? Are you a member of the Investment Management Consultants Association (IMCA)? Are you an Accredited Investment Fiduciary Auditor (AIFA)? What is your investment process? What is your investment philosophy?"

Bromelkamp's consulting group considers professional education and professional designations important to the job and hope that consumers will learn to look for advanced training when they search for financial advisors.

In an effort to assist all prospective clients in their understanding of the investment process, Donald C. DeWees Jr., senior vice president-investments of DeWees Investment Consulting Group of Wachovia Securities (Greenville, DE), presents them with a 27-page informational white paper. (Many of his concepts are referenced throughout this book.) He also advises investors to "Sit down and interview your [advisor] candidates – try to dig into their core beliefs, what their investment process is. You also need to find out whether the advisor is sales- or process-driven, and the advisor needs to articulate what the process is. If he or she can't articulate it, then there probably isn't a process, and they're probably not the type of advisor you would want to work with."

A Personalized Approach

When you interview an advisor, he/she should explain his/her process to you as well as provide a synopsis of it in writing.

Jack Krapf, along with partners Douglas Aldridge, and Clifford Johnson, Aldridge, Johnson & Krapf of Wachovia Securities (Macon, GA), provide this overview of their portfolio-management process within their brochure: "We offer a highly personalized approach to portfolio management, tailoring each client's plan to help meet his or her individual needs. Bringing this plan to life requires a highly disciplined investment process that starts with our first meeting."

There are six distinct phases to the Aldridge, Johnson & Krapf process, summarized here:

1. *Discovery* – understanding the specific needs and objectives of their clients.

2. *Strategy* – focuses on current holdings and presenting an investment roadmap.

3. *Implementation* – assets are moved to the most appropriate ve-

hicles in the most tax-efficient manner.

4. *Monitoring* – continued oversight and review of the investments.

5. *Review* – regular reviews of your portfolio and financial plan.

6. *Fine Tuning* – making needed adjustment.

A Structured Approach

In reviewing his process, which has been refined and used with more than 350 clients, Frederick Dawson emphasizes many of these same points. Describing his process, he says, "We have multiple meetings with our clients. The first one is what we call the concept interview. During this time we outline what it is we do, how we do it, when we do it and how much we charge. We also explain who in our firm is involved in the process. I like to demonstrate, by example, some of the things that might be a conflict of interest and how we transition from the planning stage and into the implementation phase. At the end of the meeting, I generally give them a checklist of data and documents we need from them, an expense sheet and our corporate ADV[1] form."

Dawson continues, "To prepare for the second meeting, we have them compile the data we requested at the first meeting. At the beginning of the second meeting, I tell them I will let them know 1) if the key elements point to them needing a financial plan, and 2) am I the right person to do it. By the end of the second meeting, I set the appropriate fee, if any, to have a financial plan prepared. At that time they are usually ready to say yes, they want to work with us."

---

1. This form is used to apply for registration as an investment advisor or to amend a registration. It consists of two parts, 1) general and personal information about the applicant, 2) information relating to the nature of the applicant's business, including basic operations, services offered, fees charged, types of clients advised, educational and business backgrounds of associates and other business activities of the applicant.

HARRIS ON INTEGRITY

"At the end of the day, trust and *integrity* are the only things that matter. If you act with *integrity* on a daily basis, your clients will always be first. Just as we trust a medical doctor, we need our clients to fully trust us to do what is best for them. We only gain this trust by acting with *integrity* at all times.

Within my practice, we strive to work only on fees and by using investments that are independent and not proprietary products. By structuring our business like this, our income and financial future is tied directly to our clients. We believe this builds trust and *integrity* in our business."

James M. Harris III, CIMA, CFP®
The Harris Group
Morgan Keegan & Co., Inc.

CHAPTER 3

PROCESS: **Prepare**
- To make ready, fit, or qualified.
- To provide with what is needed; outfit.
- To make preparations; get ready.

Finding a Competent and Trustworthy Advisor

The hypothetical story that follows was created to help you understand what you need to know to find a competent advisor. Although fictitious, this scenario sets the stage for much of this book.

John and Jane inherit $25 million from a great aunt, and go from rags to riches. After paying off a small amount of debt and meeting relatives they never knew existed, they want to invest their money wisely. They are well aware that most people who come into sudden wealth lose it very quickly. (Just consider the statistics of what happens to lottery winners. It's reported that 80 percent file for bankruptcy within five years of receiving their "big win.") They want to avoid making the same mistakes others have made. They don't have any wealthy friends to get advice from and realize that the phone calls they've received from every Tom, Dick, and Harry offering advice and service can't all be legitimate. And even if they were, how do they decide which "professional" is the right one for them?

John and Jane seek advice from their local banker. The president of the small Savings & Loan enthusiastically greets them and describes all the services the bank has available, from CDs to mutual funds. Wisely, they also visit with their H&R Block accountant for some ideas on how to invest their money and avoid paying additional taxes. The accountant suggests municipal bonds and some other investment and tax approaches. They then visit local branches of three brokerage firms and larger banks only to discover that *every one* of the advisors they meet is a "personal wealth manager" or can put them in contact with the right team of people who "do this wealth management stuff all the time." What a dilemma. Consider the following questions:

- What should this couple do?
- How do they find the right advisor?
- What skills, knowledge and experience should the advisor have?
- What investment approach should they take?
- What are the best solutions to their problems?

In reality, these same issues are faced by many investors, regardless of the amount of money involved or their sophistication level. While there are no absolute answers, it can pay to follow the advice and guidelines provided in this chapter. The advice comes from financial services experts, advisors, and industry credentialing organizations. Topics include:

- Establishing financial goals.
- Finding the right advisor(s).
- Getting referrals and checking references.
- Questions advisors should ask you, and vice-versa.
- Checking credentials.

Developing Trust

Ultimately, you should choose an advisor based upon the trust equation, which is determined, in part, by your personal comfort level with an advisor. Your confidence in an advisor will increase (or decrease) as you learn about the experiences of other clients in situations similar to your own. By understanding the processes that should be involved, and knowing about industry best practices and standards, you will be able to reasonably determine whether to employ a particular person, team, or organization in helping you attain your long-term objectives.

Most of the advisors in this book agree that many investors do not know what to look for in an advisor. Too often investors are "babes in the woods" and have no way to evaluate an advisor's value, compe-

tence, or suitability. Such investors can easily fall prey to financial preda-
tors. Fortunately, you and other investors can follow several guidelines
to increase the probability of finding the right advisor.

It requires work on your part, or what we call "due diligence." It may
seem burdensome, but remember what's at stake:

- Your money.
- Your goals.
- Your financial future.
- Your future.
- Your family.
- Future generations and your legacy.

The following tips will help you find the right advisor and feel more
confident about your financial decisions.

Learn About the Industry

Adam Westphalen suggests that investors take the time and responsibility to understand how capital markets[1] work. He recognized this
need to educate consumers when he talked with a woman who couldn't
understand the need to diversify. He says, "She perceived diversification as being more 'risky' because the funds were going into more than
one company. A common example of this is when people over-allocate
their money through a qualified plan into the stock of the company
they work for. Many loyal employees feel more comfortable with a
large personal investment in the company stock versus other companies they don't know much about. This could be an unwise move. Unless you are a member of senior management, how much do you really
know about the inner workings of your employer?"

His comments are echoed by Martim DeArantes-Oliveira, who suggests that before meeting with a financial advisor, the investor should
understand a little about the financial services industry. "They need to
spend some time researching the wire houses, banks, and trust companies. They should buy a book, go online, or take a class to find out how
the market works. The worst thing a prospective client can do is come
in completely blind as to what happens in this industry and what moti-
vates the professionals," he says.

Jeffrey Thomas also suggests that people pursue some measure of
education. "I don't care if it just a three or four day workshop, or a
more sophisticated seminar, or reading. But it is one of those things

they need to do to make sure they have a foundation developed upon which they can build," he says.

Part of that education might be to better understand the relationship of risk versus reward and what to expect in terms of realistic returns. While explained more fully in Chapters 14 and 16, it is important to realize that high returns usually come with high risks. Depending upon your financial situation, it may be unwarranted to assume any more risk than you absolutely must. As shown in Chapter 15, this often stems from unrealistic expectations.

John Chiacchiero, investment advisor with Wealth Management Group of Melhado, Flynn & Associates, Inc. (Bluffton, SC), says he sometimes finds himself looking at clients who say, "I need a 15 percent return."

"That's putting the cart before the horse because we lead with financial planning to determine what they need," he says. "I always cite that the S&P 500 basically has a 75-year average annual return of 10 percent. And if we get the prospect to accept that [10 percent], indeed, is the realistic return level, it usually begets a better conversation."

Choosing An Advisor Takes Time

One of the biggest mistakes that people make is they don't dedicate enough time and effort to finding and selecting the appropriate advisor.

Certain investors seem reluctant to spend time searching for the "right" advisor. No matter how much time it takes, you need to do your homework when it comes to this particular task. The advisor you choose will set the stage for your economic future. Therefore, it is vital to choose wisely.

Evaluate Multiple Advisors

You should interview several advisors before making your final selection. To save time, create a series of questions that you want answered or an agenda that you wish to follow. (Sample questions are provided later in this chapter.) DeArantes-Oliveira suggests you treat the meeting as an interview. "A serious interview has an agenda. When institutions are looking for financial advisors and consultants, they usually do a tremendous amount of preparation and have an agenda. It's an executive search exercise. I think that the retail client should do the same thing," he says.

Westphalen agrees, "Don't take the first offer. A major responsibility is spending the time to interview people and gain a level of comfort in understanding what they do, how they do it, how they think about the business. Just because someone has a certain designation doesn't mean anything; perhaps they are good at reading and taking a multiple choice exam."

The advisor you choose should have the experience and designations necessary to work with your financial situation. (Chapter 17 de scribes the differences between many professional designations, the continuing education requirements needed to maintain the designation, and how to check an advisor's credentials.)

Ask Peers for Referrals

When it comes to matters of wealth, you want to get referrals from people who are in a financial position similar to yours or from people who are knowledgeable about financial services professionals.

Donald DeWees Jr., whose new clients come to him mainly from referral sources or word of mouth, suggests investors consult with their family, friends, and neighbors, and talk with their accountant and lawyer.

Brent E. Bentrim, founder and managing principal, Carolopolis Family Wealth Management

Jeffrey B. Thomas, JD, CPA, CIMC, Raymond James Financial Services, discusses the need for a personal interview and asking a lot of questions. He said, "No tool/approach is fool-proof. Nothing replaces personal interviews, regardless of how the initial introduction is made. Many investors will draw comfort from questions probing an advisor's trustworthiness, and not trying to ascertain his/her competence.

Professional designations are helpful to assure that the individual is knowledgeable; CIMA and CFP® are two widely accepted professional designations serving individuals and small institutions. But, designations don't complete the picture of the advisor's priorities in life.

Don't be afraid to probe into an advisor's personal life and experiences. Is he/she willing to share his/her philosophy on matters that are important to you: Religious faith, family history and personal involvement, outside activities, contributions to one's profession, etc. Be prepared, before the interview, to put together a list of questions that you would want to ask you daughter's boyfriend if he were to propose marriage to your daughter.

Make sure the advisor can give specific examples of personal incidences that support a conclusive statement. It's not enough for someone to say: "I'm a good Dad." Delve deeper into circumstances that support that conclusion. You're seeking someone to handle your financial future. Make sure you are comfortable that this individual's life priorities are matched appropriately with your own. This is an interview approach every investor should use."

(Charleston, SC), cautions investors who turn to family or friends for advice that they may be doing themselves a large disservice by asking non-professionals. "Everyone has different goals; they need to go to somebody who really has expertise in what they are trying to accomplish." He explains that each advisor has particular strengths and weaknesses. He is candid about his own personal strengths and weaknesses. "I do a very poor job with people who are trying to accumulate wealth; however, I do a very good job with people who already have wealth and want to deal with multigenerational issues." That is, his emphasis is on wealth retention rather than wealth creation.

Bentrim is also concerned that clients aren't savvy enough to understand the different styles of firms and advisors because they've been trained to be product-oriented. "The biggest problem clients face is that large firms are constantly marketing product-based solutions and, as such, clients become very product-oriented [because that's all they've ever experienced]. Quite frankly, clients have no means or experience to figure out whether their advisor is competent or not."

Ask Professionals for Referrals

An estate or trust attorney usually has a network of other professions to draw upon. You probably wouldn't ask a criminal lawyer for the name of a good insurance agent or wealth management team because you wouldn't expect them to know. Therefore, only ask someone "in the know."

Going a step further, DeWees advises against contacting financial advisors who advertise to find business. He explains, "A successful advisor is probably not advertising (or looking for business) because their business is already at a healthy size and they are selectively growing their business through referrals. A referral-only practice is a sign of a very healthy financial advisory practice."

While this may be true for some advisors, there are many other advisors who haven't reached that point in their practice yet or may be new to a certain area. In this case, advertising may be a practical way to help build a business.

Other Potential Sources of Referrals

In addition to asking reliable sources for referrals, consider contacting the financial editors of newspapers or magazines dealing with issues similar to yours— a pension magazine, for example. Other potential sources include the Chamber of Commerce, Bar Association, successful business owners in your area, and various industry associations, many of which have local chapters. A few phone calls can lead to some excellent referrals.

Remember to interview multiple advisors. Visit with wealth specialists at banks and brokerage firms to evaluate their services, and as part of your interview, ask them who their competitors are—then visit them! Don't sign on the dotted line with anyone until you've done your homework. You have a lot at stake, just like John and Jane.

Questions to Ask

The Certified Financial Planner (CFP®) Board of Standards, Inc. developed a helpful brochure entitled "10 Questions to Ask When Choosing a Financial Planner,"[2] (or almost any type of financial advisor) and includes an interview checklist. The suggested questions below were strongly influenced by this brochure.

According to the Board of Standards, "You may be considering help from an investment advisor for a number of reasons, whether it's deciding to buy a new home, planning for retirement or your children's education, or simply not having the time or expertise to get your finances in order.

"These questions will help you interview and evaluate several financial planners to find the one that's right for you. You will want to select a competent, qualified professional with whom you feel comfortable, one whose business style suits your financial planning needs."

Here is a condensed version of the form.

Ask an advisor questions such as:

1. What experience do you have? How long have you been in business? What types of people or companies do you work with? Describe your work experience relative to your current services?

2. What are your qualifications? Ask what qualifies the advisor to offer financial advice and what professional designations are held. Ask how the advisor keeps current with industry changes. Verify that any designations held are current.

3. What services do you offer? Services depend on a number of factors including credentials, licenses, and areas of expertise. Selling insurance or securities products each require different licenses. What services do you *not* offer?

4. What is your approach to financial advice? What types of clients do you like to work with? Are you a generalist or a specialist? Make sure the advisor's viewpoint on investing is not too cautious or overly aggressive for you. Find out if the advisor will carry out the financial recommendations developed for you or refer you to others who will do so.

5. Will you be the only person working with me? If the advisor uses the services of other professionals, such as attorneys, tax specialists, insurance agents, get a list of their names to check on their backgrounds. Find out if you will be working directly with a client-relationship manager. If so, who is it? When will you meet him/her?

6. How will I pay for your services? Advisors can be paid in several ways:

   a. A salary. The advisor's company receives fees or commissions from you or others in order to pay the advisor's salary.

   b. Fees charged on an hourly rate or a flat, one time fee, which may be based on your level of wealth or the difficulty of the project.

   c. Commissions paid by you or others.

   d. Combination of fees and commissions. Some advisors may offset some portion of the fees you pay if they receive commissions for carrying out their recommendations.

   e. Fee-based advisors charge a percentage of assets under management only – there are no fees for setting up a financial plan to meet your investment objectives.

7. How much do you typically charge? Get an estimate of the possible costs involved. Could anyone besides me benefit from your recommendations? This may identify any conflicts of interest. Get it in writing. Do they get any referral fees for recommending you to others? If so, who are they and how much do they receive?

8. Have you ever been publicly disciplined for any unlawful or unethical actions in your professional career? Ask which organizations the advisor is regulated by, and contact these groups to

conduct a background check. (See Chapter 17)

9. Can I have it in writing? Ask the advisor to provide you with a written agreement that details the services that will be provided. Keep this document in your files for future reference.

Involve Other Professionals

It may be helpful to have one or more of your professional advisors with you at the meetings when you ask these or other pertinent questions. DeArantes-Oliveira points out that these experts can help you in your search [for a wealth manager]. "Your accountant and attorney should be there when you do the search. What you're doing is building a team, and the team has to be compatible. For the high-net-worth individual, the search is a lot more complex and involves a lot more personalities than just you and the consultant," he says.

Get and Check References

When asked, "How do you know if an advisor has integrity, is ethical, and is competent?" the majority of advisors agreed that getting and checking references is an important step. James M. "Jay" Harris III, senior vice president, The Harris Group of Morgan Keegan (Albany, GA), stresses: "Ask them for references—five to 10 different people. Not only ask for references, but actually go the extra mile and call them." He also suggests the investor ask questions such as:

- What were/are your objectives

- Does the advisor help you meet those objectives?

- Does he/she put you in investments that you are comfortable with?

- For conservative investors, did he/she put you in anything that was risky?

Now that you know how to find an advisor, read the next two chapters to find out what you should expect to hear from an advisor during an initial meeting.

---

1. The markets where capital, such as stocks and bonds, are traded.

2. The consumer toll free number is 800-237 6295, or visit the website at www.CFP.net

ABRAMS ON INTEGRITY

"**A** financial planner often develops a long-term relationship with a client that encompasses a significant 'mother lode' of information regarding the financial affairs and values of the client. During such a relationship, the financial planner is challenged on an on-going basis to provide a 'road map' that is consistent with the client's financial objectives, personal values, stage of life, family lifestyle, etc. The *integrity* of the financial planner plays a pivotal role in the integration of objectives, the comprehension and relevance of appropriate issues to consider, as well as the implementation and review of agreed upon courses of action. *Integrity* is the 'glue' which bonds the client to the planner. With it, there is a bond that potentially enables the relationship to proceed unabated for many years into the future. I strive in my practice to act in a manner that provides the highest level of *integrity* possible via continuing edu-

cation, the elimination of potential conflicts of interest, and the desire to provide, to the best of my ability, professional guidance.

Jacques "Jack" Abrams, CFP®, CIMC
Abrams Financial Management

CHAPTER 4

Identifying Long-Term Goals and Objectives

The previous chapter provided a series of steps that you can take to find an appropriate advisor or advisory team to help you meet your overall financial goals and objectives. But, that assumes you have a clear idea of exactly what you want your money to do for you and your family. Without a clear understanding of what you want and need in your financial future, it would be impossible to determine whether a particular advisor can assist you in getting it.

Knowing what you want your money to do for you and your family goes far beyond typical goals and objectives such as, "I want my money to grow," "I want to retire comfortably and travel around the world," and "We want Sara to go to an Ivy League school." While these are worthwhile goals, they are much too vague and don't encompass the full realm of possibilities. Remember, financial goals are usually a means to an end.

It is important to give thought to numerous personal, family and financial issues before even meeting with an advisor. A good advisor will help you further identify and define your goals and then help you construct a plan to achieve them. But, it all starts with you knowing where you want to go. Metaphorically, you are the owner of a ship. You decide where to go, and the captain and the crew (financial and professional advisors) determine how to get you there.

It is also important to do some contingency planning, that is, allow for unexpected obstacles or situations. Reginald A.T. Armstrong, president of Armstrong Wealth Management Group (Florence, SC), employs an approach that he calls "3-D Planning." Below, he deals with a couple of typical goals, and then brings up additional possibilities that many investors fail to consider – until it's too late.

Reginald A.T. Armstrong, president and client wealth manager of the Armstrong Wealth Management Group shares his system for helping investors achieve their goals: "When investors sit down to set their goals, they need to look at their dreams, the dollars and the deadlines. We call this planning in 3-D. The *dreams* are what they want, the *dollars* are how much it will cost, and the *deadline* is: When are we going to need it to happen? Retirement, or any goal, is nothing more than a cash flow. It's an outflow. You have to know when the cash outflows are going to hit. By planning in 3-D your retirement, or college funding, or even estate planning, it really helps to crystallize it. That's the first thing investors need to do.

Next, will your children and/or grandchildren have the educational opportunity you want them to have? When you talk to a retiree with six grandchildren, they want to do something for them, but they're afraid they don't even have enough for themselves. That's when it comes back to 3-D planning. What do you want to do? What is the dream? What college do they plan on sending them to, what is the deadline, and how does it affect their cash flow? With a comprehensive financial plan, we compare the cash flow they have for their retirement need, and then we throw in the extras, e.g., cash requirement for college for grandchildren. Then we find out, can they do that, and how will it affect their primary goal – retirement?

Another important question today is, will you be economically responsible for your parents? We live in a sandwich generation where many adults may have to, simultaneously, pay for college and parental care. The question is, will they be responsible and will they have the dollars to do it?

An old statistic from the Alzheimer's Association is that 40 percent of 80-year-olds and 50 percent of 85-year-olds have this horrible disease. The average lifetime cost of an Alzheimer's patient several years ago was $174,000, but it is probably higher now. If you are an only child, do you plan on your parents possibly going on Medicaid, or will you be financially responsible for them? At a cost of $3-$4 thousand a month, that's a lot to think about. Just imagine entering retirement, funding your children's college and oh, by the way, now I need to help out mom. That's where we find most investors have challenges that [they] haven't calculated necessary cash flows. What we try to do is the 3-D model for each of those questions, and then we lay it out using software.

Finally, a small percentage of my clients have sufficient assets and we ask them, is there an institution they would support if they could? We help them see how much of their assets they can afford to gift."

You'll notice it is important to look at your financial situation from many angles. Considering the "outcome of the outcome" is another way of describing it. If you contribute money to a charitable foundation, for example, how might that affect educating great grandchildren? Alternately, how will your legacy plans be furthered if you contribute additional money to a particular cause? Additional lifestyle and legacy questions are presented later in the chapter.

The Discovery

To help with the process of identifying precisely what you want your money to accomplish, Adam Westphalen provides a "Discovery Book" to clients and asks them to carefully answer the questions prior to the first meeting with him. Here are a few of his "discovery" questions.

- What about your current circumstances is motivating you to seek advice and counsel?

- What is important about money to you? Why?

- What are your primary financial goals and objectives?

- Where would you like to be five years from now?

- Time horizon?

- Percentage of assets allocated to each goal?

- Risk tolerance(s)?

In addition to questions such as these, he also asks for specific financial data to give him an overview before delving into many additional questions.

Brent Bentrim also wants to find out what is most meaningful to his clients. He focuses on helping clients define their ideal life. What makes his clients happy? What do they value? What are their strengths and weaknesses? Where do they want to be – not the dollar amount, *but what's important to them*? Is it educating their grandchildren or taking a cruise? How will this money be used over the long term? Too often clients think about these questions in nebulous terms. They may think about retiring but are not sure how to get to from point A to point B. Bentrim helps his clients develop specific, actionable goals and objectives that will get them from one point to the next.

Your advisor should be asking you questions that you haven't already considered, from "What if?" questions to "outcome of the outcome" questions. If you already have the answer(s), great! If not, the advisor may have helped you avoid a potential landmine.

James N. "Jim" Whiddon, president and chief executive officer of JWA Financial Group, Inc. (Dallas, TX), says he commonly asks couples simple financial questions, only to have them look at each other as though they'd never considered it. The question could be as basic as, "When are we going to retire?" or "What kind of after-tax budget do we need to retire on?" Another common question is, "Are we going to leave the kids anything and, if so, how much?" As Whiddon indicates, these are issues people don't talk about very often until they are forced to. And many times it's the financial advisor who confronts them with these issues.

The advisors in this book all emphasized that their success in helping their clients hinges on obtaining this critical information. Gathering this in-depth information truly differentiates them from their competitors and is vital to helping clients identify, define, and achieve their financial goals.

Things to Consider

The questions below are derived from two sources [1] and are designed to assist investors with important goals prior to choosing an investment advisor. Keep in mind that not all types of financial advisors will ask you these or similar questions because their business focus may be different. Nevertheless, it is important for you to know the answer these questions.

When teaching advisors how to offer higher-level advice, they are told that "it is not enough to merely financially profile your client." You want to ask thought-provoking, revealing questions such as those listed below. Many of these are close-ended questions requiring a simple, short answer. Whenever possible, however, try to answer the "how" and "why" (open-ended) questions. This will provide the advisor greater insight into your personality, values, and objectives.

Values

What principles, values, and virtues are most important to you? Why? How and with whom do you intend to share them? Some clients may want to share with their immediate family, others the world. Asking how a person wishes to be remembered and why often adds valuable insight.

Family/Community/Country/World

What things in your family, community, country, or world would you like to change, preserve, protect or re-establish? How important is this to you, and how do you intend to accomplish this? What resources will be employed to assist you?

People

Whom in your life do you most want to impact? Why and how? What are the most effective ways to do so? What procedures do you have in place, or intend to put into place, to help ensure that your wishes are fulfilled?

Approaches and Vehicles

Do you want "hands-on" control, or do you wish to empower other people or organizations (community, charity, political, etc.) that are pursuing similar ends?

Resources

How much time, effort and money are you willing or able to devote to the accomplishment of your goals? What are your priorities? What additional internal and external resources can you enlist to support your efforts?

Support Resources

Who can you turn to for help, support or guidance in the dynamic execution of your life goals? How will they help you? What else can they do? Why are they doing it?

Tell the "Doctor" Everything

You must provide your advisor with all of the information you can about your situation. Full disclosure is vital, and advisors agree that this is an important component of the overall process. DeWees Investment Consulting Group's Donald DeWees Jr. says it best: "I will not work with clients unless they reveal all their financial information. It is part of the trust equation, and they have to be perfectly honest with me. I'm the money-doctor. You cannot withhold from me critical information that is going to help me make a complete and accurate diagnosis of your situation."

George Connell Jr., president and chief investment officer, Washington Investment Advisors (Radnor, PA), tells us he finds his clients are basically focused on the following concepts:

1. *Keeping what they've got* For example, they sold a business, which created a huge financial windfall in their lives. All of a

sudden they have a lot of money, so protecting it is first and foremost

2. *Making more.* They are of an entrepreneurial spirit. They've had some success. They want continued success, and they don't want anything to hamper that.

3. *Proper distribution of wealth over their lifetime.*

4. *Proper distribution of their wealth* if they are incapacitated or die.

Like these clients, you need to share the concepts that are a priority in your life with your financial advisor.

Ira Rapaport says since most of his clients already have a significant net worth, "Their number one goal is to preserve their wealth and develop a well-diversified portfolio that is consistent with their overall financial plan." You must determine your objectives so your advisor can develop a financial plan around your particular needs.

In Conclusion

Having successfully transitioned his business to a fee-only advice practice in 1996, Jeffrey Thomas reminds investors that the steps for developing financial goals are dictated by the stage of life in which investors find themselves. "They are closely tied and dictated by life's other goals, priorities and desires, such as how one handles saving for a down payment on the first home, or putting money away for their children's college expenses," he says. "How one handles money, and the procedures for developing the steps are inextricably connected to answering the questions: What is the money going to be used for and when will I need it? What are my concerns about achieving that goal?"

---

1. *The Mega Producers: Secrets of Financial Services Superstars to Lead You to the Top,* by Steven Drozdeck (Dearborn Trade Publishing, 2003), and the Macro Strategic Planning™ course developed by Bruce Wright, author of *The Wright Exit Strategy: Wealth. How to Create It, Keep It, and Use It* (Sammi Press, 1997). The former is recommended reading for financial advisors; the latter is recommended for both financial advisors and investors.

Rapaport on Integrity

" *Integrity* is one of the most important qualities I strive to maintain. Each client relationship is built on trust, honesty, timely communication, and the assurance that I am truly adding value through prudent, objective advice. My clients are entrusting me with far more than their financial assets. Their personal dreams and aspirations, and even the well-being of their families, are in my hands.

I feel honored that my clients place a high degree of confidence in my judgment, knowing that I am fully committed to guiding them through all stages of their financial lives. Without the element of *integrity*, my clients cannot be certain that I am working with only their best interests in mind."

Ira Rapaport. CPA/PFS, CIMA, CFP®
RINET Company, LLC

PROCESS: **Research**
- Studious, systematic investigation or inquiry to ascertain, uncover, or assemble facts, used as a basis for conclusions or the formulation of theory.
- To do research on or for.

Research & Review:
The First Meeting

Your initial meeting with a financial advisor allows each party to get to know and assess each other. It is important that you, and any other professional advisors who accompany you, feel comfortable with the financial advisor on a personal level and that the advisor feels comfortable with you.

In addition, the advisor's investment philosophy or approach should make sense to you. What are they helping you accomplish? James Harris III says the best way to make money is to not lose money; and the best way to not lose money is to put it into three to five different asset categories and rebalance on a regular basis. If you were to choose Harris as your financial advisor, this logical advice should make sense to you on a gut level.

While you may not be able to judge a person's competency, you can get a feel for them as people — whether they seemed concerned about you or whether they seemed to put you through a cookie-cutter analysis. Did they ask a lot of questions and actually listen to the answers? Did they answer your questions and make sure that you understood the answers? All of these factors allow you to intuitively know whether this advisor is right for you. Remember that this is "the honeymoon stage." If they are not making a good impression on you before you become a client, then don't assume that they will change later on.

You must take into consideration that you may not "click" with extremely competent advisors just because of personality differences. That's why it's wise to have a range of advisors to choose from.

Most advisors in this book agree that you need to meet with a few advisors and check for personality matches. You should ask about an advisor's long-term business plans, such as how large the organization may be in the next five to 10 years. You may not want to get lost in the shuffle of a large-scale operation. The size of your account should match the size of other accounts handled by the advisor. For example, you don't want to be someone's biggest client. Why? Because if the advisor only deals with smaller clients – presumably with less demanding needs – that advisor may not have the sophistication level you need. Conversely, if you are one of the smaller clients, you must question the level of service and attention you will receive. This does not always happen, but it is something to consider.

Similarly, just because an advisor has one or more professional designations, doesn't automatically make him/her the best person for the job. Some advisors joke about having so many designations behind their names that it looks like alphabet soup. As you'll see in Chapter 17, different designations connote different skills and competencies. If an advisor doesn't have the designation(s), he/she should have access to people with the required knowledge. Chapter 12 includes information on multi-disciplinary teams.

Setting the Stage

The first meeting or interview is the time to get to know your advisor on a personal level and vice-versa, and the time to begin a professional relationship.

Here are a few things you can expect an advisor to discuss or provide for you at the initial or follow-up meeting:

1. Ask a lot of questions about your personal goals, financial goals, understanding of the markets, the names and functions of your other advisors (attorney, accountant, insurance agent, etc.). Use the "10 Questions to Ask When Choosing a Financial Planner" from Chapter 4.

2. Explain his/her financial planning and/or investment process.

3. Introduce you to other members of the professional team.

4. Discuss reasonable expectations regarding service, market returns, etc.

5. Explain costs of services and the limits of his/her services.

6. Provide legal documentation that reflects any agreements and projected costs.

7. Describe office team members and any other strategic relationships with other professionals.

8. Introduce you to the office team members who you will be interacting with.

9. Describe his/her qualifications.

Criteria for Selecting an Advisor

Each advisor in this book offers some insights into how to evaluate a potential advisor. You'll note that the next five questions are ways of asking, "Is this the person or team that I am willing to entrust my future to?"

Is he/she adding value? A 20-year veteran of the industry, George Connell Jr. suggests you ask yourself if this financial advisor is going to add value to the overall equation. "When prospects ask me this question, I tell them what I do is not very complicated, but maintaining the discipline to do what I do is." Investing should be an unemotional process but often ends up being an emotional process. Therefore, you must have an advisor who takes the time to remind you of the goals you set. If those expectations or goals change over time, then your advisor must take those changes into consideration.

Is the system right for me? Considering himself a consumer advocate, James Whiddon explains that occasionally a client, after seeing his system, will simply decline to use his services. Sometimes they may not want to pay an upfront, flat fee for a financial plan. As Whiddon says, "The fact that they don't want to pay for the plan speaks to their level of commitment, about how serious they are about getting their house in order financially." Some clients may just be looking for a sounding board on investment decisions. Whiddon continues, "When communicating to prospective clients, we want to be efficient in two ways: 1) attracting clients, and 2) repelling clients. We don't want anything in between. The way to avoid the lukewarm prospect is to clearly define who you are as a firm, as a person and your process. If we clearly define those, we feel we won't have to be afraid of the results because the system is going to do what it is supposed to do. We do not try to be all things to all people." Whiddon's JWA Financial Groups are specialists in in the retirement transition niche.

Do we think alike? With a focus on financial planning and investment management, John Chiacchiero tries to help his clients understand that over time, the equity markets will likely outperform all other investment classes, including bank accounts and real estate. Investing your money in a 2 percent certificate of deposit (CD) is not going to give you the kind of return you need to meet long-term goals.

Can I work with them? Chiacchiero goes on to say, "The bottom line is, 'can you get along with this investment advisor, is the relationship so good that you can work together over a long period of time, and can you trust them?' That's why I think being honest upfront with that client is really helpful. It works for us. We follow principles that aren't new, but they have been proven to work over long periods of time."

Do they have the right experience? Harris, who started in the insurance industry in 1990 and became licensed as a financial advisor in 1993, points out that "The more objectives you have, the more problems you want to solve, the more experienced advisor you need."

Do they ask the right questions? An excellent way to determine if an advisor will add value, thinks the way you do, and is someone you can work with, is based on what questions they ask you and *how* they ask them. In Chapter 4, you were instructed to spend time answering questions about what money means to you and your family. Also, you were told that top advisors will conduct in-depth interviews, probing you about your needs and goals. So if an advisor doesn't ask you in-depth questions, you probably shouldn't work with him/her. One of the worst things an advisor can do is to quickly and conveniently label you and offer you a cookie-cutter solution to investing. Stay away from this financial assembly line approach.

In conclusion, when searching for competent professionals, meet a few candidates, interview them, and as part of your process, discover how thorough they are in interviewing you. Do they only think along narrow parameters, or do they present all possible solutions for helping you attain your dreams?

The First Meeting

ARMSTRONG ON INTEGRITY

"*Integrity* along with trust is the foundation for any successful enterprise. This is especially true in the financial services industry where you are dealing with people's life savings.

My definition of *integrity* is: You mean what you say; you do what you said you were going to do; you always do what is in the client's best interest. In our practice at the Armstrong Wealth Management Group, we strive to provide a consistent service experience so that our *integrity* is constantly reinforced."

Reginald A.T. Armstrong, RIA
Armstrong Wealth Management Group

PROCESS: **Research**
- To go over or examine again.
- To study carefully; survey or evaluate.
- To make a critical evaluation of.
- A careful study or survey.

Additional Factors to Consider
When Choosing an Advisor

Choosing an advisor is a critical course of action in determining your financial future. Because it is such an important process, this chapter is filled with additional supportive information on selecting an advisor, including:

- The Cost Factor

- Large versus Small Independent Firms

- Are Your Investment Philosophies in Sync?

- A Rational Approach

- The Team Behind the Advisor

- Do You Really Need a Financial Advisor?

The Cost Factor: *You don't get something for nothing*

While some advisors in this book offer a free, initial consultation, it would be unreasonable to expect that any professional, who has spent years of effort getting to his/her current position, would provide financial advice for free. The fee for a financial plan varies based on the time, effort, and complexity of the project. A simple plan may cost $500 while a complex plan could cost up to $10,000. Whatever you do, avoid the free or inexpensive software programs that purport to do financial planning. This is like getting medical or legal advice based on 15 simple questions.

Bassett, Brosius & Dawson's Frederick Dawson says he sets his fee by the end of the second client meeting. He explains, "At that time, they are usually ready to say yes, they want to work with us." He explains to the client that his fee gives 12 months' worth of unlimited phone calls, appointments, discussions, meetings, consultations with

A Confused Marketplace

Jack Krapf, senior vice president, and Douglas Aldridge, managing director, Aldridge, Johnson & Krapf of Wachovia Securities, elegantly described how difficult it is for investors to differentiate from one company to another. He correctly points out some of the reasons for this confusion and then identifies a key differentiating factor between typical brokers and high-level advisors.

The marketplace has become distorted, a misunderstanding about what real consulting services are about. It becomes tough for clients to really pick and choose who are the best people to work with. Traditionally, an individual, foundation, or committee is going to work with whom they like whether or not they are making the best decision. The wire houses have institutional consulting divisions that have been put in place to do two things. The first is to provide consulting services, to sell wrap-fee business to the marketplace and to allow their distribution system (the brokers) to sell them.

With the consulting divisions doing all the work, all they need to know is how to sell. That has confused the marketplace. Investors don't understand what they are buying. When looking at all these firms, they are all the same. They provide the same services and the same pricing. All these firms— wire houses, regional firms, banks, that are selling fee-based advice also have investment consulting, or wealth management groups. Many of them have spent the time to acquire the knowledge, and focus on this type of businesses. But remember, this is all we do. We have gone back to school, gotten out CIMAs, to provide these types of services. We demonstrate years of experience. Our knowledge is impressive. Ultimately, many still hire who they feel comfortable with, but hopefully with more education, the will learn to select the best advisor for the job.

Authors' Comments

While professional designations do not guarantee competence, it does demonstrate commitment to professional growth. The designations and the ethical codes associated with them are presented in chapter 17. The independent associations that provide these designations have some of the highest standards in the industry. Some of these designations require years of effort to attain, and have substantial continuing education requirements, akin to what attorney's, CPAs, and doctors must take. The same rigorous standards are not required for others within the financial services industry.

him, his staff, the attorney, and whatever else is needed. He continues, "I do give my clients the option of paying me by the hour, or to pay a flat fee. The important thing is for them to understand what it's going to cost them right upfront. In 22 years of doing business, I've never had anyone opt for the hourly fee, which is fine. I don't want my clients not to call because they think the call is going to cost them something. I like to remove all those barriers so they will communicate with me."

Remember that nothing is free. You must pay for products and services either in hidden costs or pre-established fees.

Investment Philosophy

Although covered in greater detail in Chapter 11, here are some examples of advisor thought processes.

- Clients must understand what they are trying to accomplish with their pool of assets.

- Tax consequences need to be considered.

- The need to emphasie a long term approach.

The previously referenced DeWees Investment Consulting Group informational white paper provides an excellent summary of an investment philosophy and a list of truisms that all of us should take to heart.

The DeWees Investment Consulting Group helps all types of investors crystallize their objectives, understand risk, and design and implement appropriate investment strategies. Some of the core beliefs that drive its investment philosophy are:

1. It's not what you make, but what you keep that counts.

2. Markets cycle, and everything within regresses to the mean.

3. Short-term money doesn't belong in the stock market.

4. Put at-risk money in stocks, safe money in cash and quality bonds.

5. Investors have a 3:1 loss aversion ratio (-5 percent feels like -15 percent).

6. Risk comes in many forms, but failing to meet your financial goals could be the greatest.

7. Don't take more risk than is necessary to reach your financial

goals.

8. Show us a good market timer, and we'll show you mediocre results.

9. Past performance is not indicative of future results.

10. On average, a 10-year bond will yield nearly 90 percent of a 30 year bond, with half the volatility.

11. We'll take Pete Rose over Mark McGuire any day (walks/singles/ doubles, avoid strikeouts).

12. There is no free lunch.

13. Don't fight the FED.

14. Money goes where it is treated best.

15. For taxable investors, stocks, not stock funds.

16. For all investors, bonds, not bond funds.

17. Packaged products are usually better for the issuer/seller than the client.

The Rational Approach

Beware of the advisor who promises you the sun, the moon, and the sky. Similarly, beware of demanding the sun, the moon, and the sky— you won't find competent people who will accede to that demand.

John Chiacchiero remembers a prospective client who walked away from doing business with him because their investment philosophies did not match. According to Chiacchiero, a 75-year-old gentleman walked into his office with a couple million dollars and said, "If you can't get me a 20 percent return, I don't want to talk to you." Chiacchiero proceeded to explain to him, "You don't understand the risk-reward relationship. That's not real." The man didn't do business with him, but as an Registered Investment Advisor (RIA) in a fiduciary role, Chiacchiero says, "I can't sit there and tell this person, given his age and need for income, that attempting to shoot for 20 percent was the right thing to do. It wasn't. If he finally did what he wanted me to do for him, he probably lost a good measure of it."

On the other hand, Chiacchiero tells about another client who origi- nally had about $1.2 million, lost most of it, and came to him with a portfolio of $250,000--invested in 11 technology stocks. After the meeting, she was able to understand how important it was to start looking at her expenses and what was going to be realistic moving forward. Chiacchiero shares, "Her first desire was to try to get back what she had, and I had to subtly work around that over a couple of weeks until she finally accepted that it probably wasn't going to happen. The question then became, can we make what is left last the rest of her life and grow it a bit?"

These two stories underscore the need for realistic expectations. In all probability, the 75-year-old man got caught up in "herd psychology" and the belief that great markets will continue forever. The woman's investment plan certainly lacked diversification and took a huge loss. Wisely, she came to the realization that a 500 percent increase ($250,000 appreciating to $1,200,000 is approximately a five-fold increase) was unrealistic and chose a safer course of action.

The Team Behind You

A major difference between large firms and independent ones is the service received, as well as whether the team has a vested interest in your success. James Whiddon points out that investors may receive even higher levels of service at a smaller firm.

Many of the prospects coming to Whiddon had been disillusioned with large brokerage firms. Whiddon believes that most clients initially go to a large firm because they believe they have the entire firm working for them. In reality, clients of large firms do not necessarily have a team working for them, just one individual and perhaps an assistant and resources within that firm. But an independent firm is truly a team. All clients are the firm's clients, just as they would be in a law firm. So the irony is that many times the small independent firms really offer a larger team than a larger firm would, and all of their team members have a vested interest in servicing the client.

Go It Alone?

Ultimately each client must make an important decision: Do I do it myself or use the services of a professional? Consider these three analogies when deciding whether you want to be a do-it-yourself investor.

Douglas Aldridge, of Aldridge, Johnson & Krapf, shares this analogy: "If an individual wants to take care of their own yard, they don't need a gardener. It's the same thing with financial expertise. If someone wants to do the research themselves, they don't need a consultant," he says. "There are a lot of tools out there. It just depends on how much time they are willing to spend on it. Although the investor may not understand the total process, they can still make money. They just have to buy the right stocks, the right mutual funds and be in the right sectors at the right time. With luck they can hit a home run. However, most investors are not content to leave their financial futures to luck. That's why clients hire us."

Whiddon uses a medical analogy. "If you go to a shoulder doctor for an operation, you want to make sure she has done the exact operation numerous times. The same holds true when selecting a financial advisor. Eighty to 90 percent of our clients are either retired or transitioning into retirement now, and many will retire within five years. Why would a client who is going through retirement transition select a firm that specializes in a younger demographic when they know we are servicing clients just like them all the time."

Using Home Depot as an example, Chiacchiero explains that everything you need to build a house is at their store; you don't have to go anywhere else. "The question is, 'Can you build a house?' You may understand some of the basics – frames, windows, and so forth – but can you build it? And, more importantly do you want to? I look at our process in the same light. The information is everywhere, but do you know how to put that information together in a plan that is suitable for you?"

In Conclusion

When choosing an advisor it is important to have specific criteria, correctly evaluate the situation, and remain objective. Search for people who ask the hard questions, suggest a conservative, rational approach and don't tell you what you want to hear.

Additional Factors to Consider

THOMAS ON INTEGRITY

"*Integrity* means putting the client's interest first in every circumstance in your dealing with their financial affairs. Sometimes that means not making a sale or accepting deposits if it is not in their best interests or consistent with their comfort levels. I have recommended people pay down the debt on their homes rather than invest funds during this bear market. I've also recommended that people investigate a guaranteed *pre-paid* college savings program in addition to a 529 savings plan, even though I do not personally profit from such an approach.

An agreed-upon strategic, asset-allocation approach is critical to a client's understanding of what will happen to his/her portfolio over time. In calm waters, every ship has a good captain. Having a written Investment Policy Statement keeps them on track during the stormy periods. A simple, targeted, diversified, and understandable approach lets my clients sleep at night.

Jeffrey B. Thomas, JD, CPA, CIMC
Raymond James Financial Services

CHAPTER 7

PR**O**CESS: **Objective**
• A goal or purpose, as of a mission or assignment.
• Creating of or representing facts or reality without reference to feelings or opinions.
• Not prejudiced; unbiased. Impersonal, detached, disinterested, fair-minded.

Objectives:
Defined, Refined and Formalized

A ll of the above definitions for the word "objective" apply to investing and working on a financial plan, but the first one is most important. During the objective-setting step of the process, an advisor should help you further identify and refine the goals that you had previously outlined. They do this by carefully listening to you and then asking additional questions to help refine your objectives. Some goals may have a leverage effect on other goals, while others may be contradictory. Some goals may even be unrealistic. During this process, the advisor should take good notes to ensure he/she understands you and to make sure that pertinent information doesn't slip through the cracks. The advisor will help categorize those objectives in order of importance. From this information, a financial plan will be prepared that will direct the process toward the attainment of your goals.

The most important point to remember during your discussions with an advisor is:

Your objectives are the guiding and driving factor for the entire investment process.

According to Carolopolis Family Wealth Management's Brent Bentrim, investors do not always know precisely what they need to accomplish their goals. However, they do have goals they want to accomplish. So, it becomes the advisor's responsibility to perform the appropriate diagnostics and create the plan. Bentrim uses an analogy of an auto mechanic. "It's like taking your car to the garage when it's making a bumping noise. The mechanic will say you need this and this and that. What do you do? We don't want the mechanic to ask us to make every little decision. The decision really has to be made by the expert. We want him to tell us to bring the car in and it'll be ready after 1 p.m. It's similar in our business. You have to run a diagnostic before tinkering under the engine."

Bentrim is often invited to present to groups on "The Power of the Endorphin Zone: How to Retire and Thrive on Your Terms." Typically, from those sessions, eight to 10 couples are interested in attending his half-day interactive workshop that will clarify their vision of an ideal life. With a real passion to help people reach their maximum potential, Bentrim says, "I think they become clients not so much because they understand the importance of a plan and discipline to implement their vision, but mainly they want to continue to be associated with a qualified professional who has passion for helping them realize their dreams, and does not view them (the client) as a buying unit."

Getting to Know You

Jacques S. "Jack" Abrams, president and founder of Abrams Financial Management (Wellesley, MA), says at the initial financial planning meeting, he purposely uses a fairly unstructured approach with new clients. He feels that if he has people fill out biographical questionnaires ahead of time, it leads him too far down the road to what the possible answer(s) might be. He explains, "I initially like to meet a client with a 'blank sheet' and hopefully as a good listener. For one to two hours, I have them talk about themselves, e.g., where they grew up; a description of their family as it relates to parents, siblings and family values; a biographical overview of their professional and/or personal activities; an assessment of their career status; their objectives; major issues impacting their lives; what answers they're seeking as a result of the financial planning process, etc. If the client is reticent to discuss something, that's fine."

He continues, "At the conclusion of the first session, I ask the client to provide me with various financial documents, e.g., tax returns, insurance policies, estate documents, etc. At that time, I try to get an initial sense of whether the things they've discussed at the initial meeting complement their financial situation. It's quite possible that they may appear to be going down a different 'road' than the goals they've discussed at the initial meeting. In addition, it's my challenge to consider each of their goals as 'given' but often there will be inconsistencies between them. Consequently, there is a need for the client to recognize they might have to consider tradeoffs. In future meetings, as the preliminary plan is being developed I have to tell them, 'Look, here are some inconsistencies, so we're going to have to make some adjustments.'"

It's also important to apply sound investment and protection principles to allow for unexpected illnesses, accidents, emergency expenses, and other contingencies. Consider that there are approximately 40,000 automotive deaths in the United States each year. With the rare exception of drivers bent on suicide, not one of the others "planned" on having an accident that day. If they were underinsured, their families may be in deep financial trouble. Even more prevalent is the number of accidents that result in temporary or permanent disabilities. Consider the cost of long-term health care for Alzheimer's, cancer and other diseases. How about the costs of old age?

It is the job of your financial advisor to bring up these possibilities and ensure that you are adequately covered. According to James Harris III, the net result is a customized plan suitable for your particular situation. You benefit from the structure as well as the flexibility of the process, and you decide how much personal involvement you want in the process.

A Peace of Mind

Abrams likes to look at life insurance as a safeguard for those unexpected occurrences. He tells a could-have-been tragic story about a client who, unexpectedly, in his late 30s had a life-threatening form of cancer. It occurred in a relatively short period of time. Fortunately, at a meeting with the client and his wife several months before the diagnosis, Abrams had recommended the client consider purchasing a life insurance policy to provide protection for his wife and young children.

According to Abrams, "They followed my advice and obtained coverage. During the chemotherapy and radiation treatments, they thanked me for the peace of mind the life insurance provided as they focused their attention on the more important matter of him getting better (which he did). I don't think that just managing investments can fill all of the client's needs, especially when you are dealing with individuals. You don't have the luxury to say, 'I'm an investment advisor and I just manage money.' The clients are real people; they have real faces and lives. You need to integrate investments as one component of an overall comprehensive, congruent financial plan. You shouldn't by default eliminate all of these 'life factors' and only consider the investment component."

A previous chapter described Reginald Armstrong's "Planning in 3-D" where dreams, dollars, and deadlines are considered. It's important to go further by asking additional sophisticated and important questions such as: 1) Do you have a plan designed to triple your income during retirement? The truth is, people are retiring earlier, and living longer. According to the latest statistics, 75 percent of the male population and 85 percent of women will live to age 65. The women will have an additional life expectancy of 20 years, on average. That's a lot of people who need to plan for a long retirement—perhaps 20 to 30 years.

Armstrong explains, "There is a concept I use called 'personal rate of inflation.' For someone in their 30s or 40s, the rate of inflation today is about 2 percent. Things like mortgages and car payments are fairly fixed and inflation won't affect that as much. But for the retiree, the two biggest expenses are their health care and their groceries. Health care expenses go up at a much faster rate than the general rate of inflation. So, conservatively, we use a 4 percent rate of inflation when we calculate. If you have a 4 percent rate of inflation and you are expecting to live 20 to 30 years into retirement, you had better have a plan designed to triple your income during retirement."

Fuzzy words

In addition to helping clarify your life and monetary goals, a good advisor will ensure that any "fuzzy words" are clearly defined. As George Connell Jr. says, "What one client might find to be super service, another might say was very ordinary. If you're the client, be specific in terms of what it is you want and what it is you expect."

The need to have realistic expectations in determining portfolio performance will be addressed in greater detail in Chapters 14 to 16, but the concept is important to remember here as you look at and define your objectives. Like those "fuzzy words," unrealistic expectations can lead to miscommunication, mistakes, and misalignments. For example, what, specifically, does long-term growth mean to you? Is it 20 percent return per year? Is that before or after inflation? Is that growth guaranteed or is there substantial risk involved? Would a growth rate of 1 percent over inflation be satisfactory? What is the definition of long-term– five, 10, 50 years? Unless specified, terms such as growth, income, safety, protection, service, and satisfaction need to be defined early in the relationship.

Sometimes people have unrealistic, often unconscious expectations that can't be met. It is best to deal with these early on in the financial planning process than to experience disappointment later on.

Advisors should spend time eliciting your conscious and unconscious expectations on future performance and risk. Many have developed some innovative ways to do this. Yet, even these innovative methods must be supplemented with ongoing communication and education.

The Objective is Objectivity

Many advisors go to great lengths to "sit on the same side of the table as their clients." That is, they do not sell any of their firm's proprietary products, generate or share in commissions if they are purely fee-based, and may not even use certain research if there is even the remotest possibility that it may taint their thinking. This is in accordance with the ethical standards of most industry associations.

Each of the advisors interviewed for this book discuss the need for objectivity, without any apparent or potential conflict of interest (such as commissions). This was a key reason they chose a fee-based business structure and subscribe to strict codes of ethics. All financial advisors, whether fee-based or commissioned, have a responsibility to act in a client's best interest.

As John Chiacchiero states, "We do have a legal, fiduciary obligation given to us by the Securities and Exchange Commission (SEC) to act in the client's best interest. You hire a lawyer and you expect him to have no other agenda aside from giving you the best legal advice given your situation. Same thing for your accountant - you expect them to have no other hidden agenda. The same thing with a RIA firm. My desire is to provide the best guidance possible to ensure the investors meets their goals. We don't use any proprietary products. We don't sell insurance, although we may suggest insurance products as part of an overall plan. All of this is with the intent of helping our clients meet their goals."

In Conclusion

Your objectives are the guiding and driving factor for the entire investment process. While different advisors may have different approaches to gathering information, their common concern is to help you identify and define your goals. An advisor who asks a lot of questions, considers contingencies, and is absolutely clear about your objectives can help you attain those goals.

Whiddon on Integrity

"To JWA Financial Group, *integrity* means that we do what is right, in spite of the consequences, with a pure and honest dedication. A standard rule we follow in the office is simply that we do not do anything that would compromise or threaten the success that our clients are striving to achieve. This includes making sure all of our actions in the workplace, no matter how trivial, would stand up to scrutiny if our clients could witness all that we do both privately and publicly on their behalf."

James Whiddon, CFP®, ChFC, CLU
JWA Financial Group, Inc.

CHAPTER 8

PROC**ESS: Communication**
- The act of communicating; exchange of ideas, conveyance of information.
- That which is communicated, as a letter or message.

Effective Communication: A Dual Responsibility

Communication between you and your advisor is the key to a success, and a strong, long-term relationship. You should know how your investment plan is working, what the advisor is doing, the performance of any money managers, and what mid-course corrections may be necessary. In addition, you must remember to inform your advisor about any changes in your personal or financial situation, such as divorce, tax liabilities, and objective changes.

The communication process actually begins with the marketing materials that advisors distribute to clients and prospective clients. The materials convey, among other information, a mission statement, business approaches, and services available. Reputation and service quality is determined through referrals and references, by how a receptionist answers the phone, and the appearance of the office. Advisors should go to great lengths to ensure they project a clear picture of who they are and what they do.

Many high-level advisors have "relationship managers" who periodically contact each client for updates while, at the same time, updating the client about economic, market, and portfolio changes. The advisor and/or relationship manager meets with each client, depending on the size and complexity of the account, either quarterly, semi-annually, or annually. In addition, they often send out regular written updates or newsletters. Educational seminars are another component of the communication process.

An Understanding

From the advisor's perspective, it is not only important that the client is told about the communication processes, but that the client *understands* the essence of the process.

Washington Investment Advisor's George Connell Jr. explains, "It is important that there is a process, and that the advisor can describe it. Next, it's important that the client be able to say they are comfortable with the process, how the portfolio is constructed, and what expectations are reasonable for the marketplace and, therefore, this particular account."

According to Connell, the amount of communication that is required might be time intensive in the beginning and less so later. He says, "I also like to include the client's other financial professionals in conversations. I want to talk to the other trusted advisors at least once or twice a year. That's part of the process as far as I am concerned. That's how I communicate. For instance, I want our client to be fairly comfortable about going home to see her husband and saying, "I saw George today and I got a step-by-step explanation of what it is he would like to do with our account and, ultimately, how he is going to tell us if we are on target, above target, or below target, and what he is going to do about it.""

A written plan or Investment Policy Statement (IPS) should be expected from your advisor and is often required by state or federal mandates. (See Chapter 13) The plan, or IPS, is a document that spells out your investment objectives, risk tolerance(s)[1], rates of return needed, available assets and liabilities, types of managers who can be used, etc. This statement becomes the basis of everything that is done for your benefit. It is a "living document" and should be updated regularly.

Matthew N. Potter, branch manager and registered principal with Raymond James Financial Services (Cheyenne, WY), agrees. "When I get a new client, we start out meeting quarterly. Eventually they may not want to meet that often, so it becomes a couple times a year; maybe once a year will be enough for many of them. It's not always a formal review, that's okay because then I can talk to them informally about any changes that have occurred in their lives. Every time I have a review with a client, the Investment Policy Statement is on the table with us. We always go over the objectives, and I will ask if anything's changed. Then we will make any necessary changes." Because he lives in a small town he often bumps into his clients on the street and gets a quick update about any changes in their lives.

Investor Responsibilities

Investors also have certain obligations to their advisor. Not only must they inform the advisor about any personal and financial changes, they should inform the advisor about any expectations that are not being met or any change in investment objectives. Not all clients and advisor have small-town communication opportunities like Potter.

While you can wait until scheduled meetings with your advisor to update him/her on personal and financial information, there are times when it is wise to be proactive and inform the advisor as soon as possible. Such situations include:

- Birth of a child
- Change in investment objectives
- Divorce
- Death of a spouse
- Unexpected liabilities
- Taking over responsibility for a parent
- Change in the will
- Major illness

Each of the above may result in a restructuring of the investment plan, making it critical to inform your advisor quickly.

Raymond James' Jeffrey Thomas says clients will tell him, "You know I really need to get control of my debt." He is quick to remind them, "You really can't be a responsible investor until you are able to control other financial aspects of your life. It doesn't do any good to go into the market and try to generate long-term returns of 8 to 11 percent if you are paying out 20 percent to a credit card company. So first we have to get a plan in place to address these issues."

The Long-Term Approach

Major changes in you life should be dealt with immediately, but normally the long-term investment process only requires periodic shifts in strategy. Most advisors take a long-term approach and suggest that, barring unusual circumstances, you should give any money manager a full-market cycle (four to six years) to demonstrate performance. Whether you have a monthly, quarterly, semi-annual, or annual performance review depends on your individual circumstances—hence, no hard-and-fast rules. Here are a few pointers on what to expect at your performance review meeting.

First of all, how long should the meeting take? As Yogi Berra would say, "It should take as long as it takes!" But more seriously, the length of the meeting is determined by such factors as: changes in portfolio, economic or market conditions, changes in personal or financial circumstances, and how the information is delivered by your advisor. Some people simply want a condensed version, while others want an extremely detailed review. Try to get an idea of how long the meeting will take when you make the appointment so neither you nor your advisor has to leave before everything has been discussed.

Connell suggests that to make the best use of time at the meeting, an agenda should be set beforehand. "I think setting an agenda for the client-advisor meeting is important. No one likes to walk into a randomly organized meeting. Both the client and the advisor should set the agenda for the meeting to ensure specific points are covered. In my opinion, by setting a specific agenda, the odds of you having a successful meeting increase."

It is wise to write down any specific questions you might have, and you may want to send them to the advisor prior to the meeting. That gives your advisor the chance to do additional research or prepare an explanation; otherwise you may have to wait a few days or weeks for an answer.

Agenda for Client-Advisor Meetings

The typical meeting agenda might include the following:

1. Advisor will ask about any personal or financial changes in your life.

2. Advisor will review your original objectives and describe how these objectives are being met, or why they are not—at the moment. If you're not on track, the advisor will recommend needed changes.

3. Respond to any questions you may have.

4. Provide you with additional information/education.

Thomas shares a conversation he had with clients who informed him they had just received a severance package. They had both quit working, were selling their house, and moving to another state. This decision changed their financial picture significantly. Thomas explains, "We're now talking about how much cash we need to raise for a down payment on the new house and what kind of cash flow, or cash reserves they need to get them through the transition period. We hadn't talked about these possibilities two years ago, but now it's in the mix. That's why it is so important to have good communication with the financial consultant and make them aware of any changes that occur."

Frederick Dawson approaches his client meetings with a sense of humor. He's careful to make sure that his clients really understand the process and goes through great lengths to be available. "Many times I suggest to my clients that we must walk through the Garden Of Understanding. I like to have fun with people I work with. I attribute my success to the fact that I try to make this stuff fun and light. I tell my clients upfront that I'm not a very good salesperson, but I'm a pretty darn good teacher. I allow them to ask me any questions that come to mind." He also tell them the four rules right up front:

1. There is no such thing as a stupid question

2. I don't care if you have to ask me the same question 10, 15, or 20 times, that's okay.

3. I've got very thick skin. Ask me any question that comes to mind. I don't want you to think you're going to offend or challenge me.

4. If I change the rules, I'll let you know. And, if you change the rules, I expect the same courtesy in advance.

Reginald Armstrong says he doesn't revisit all the issues involving the client every time he meets with them. He explains, "If I meet with a high-net-worth client every quarter, I'll probably choose one issue to touch on. Right now we're talking with our clients about tax diversification. We're looking at how people are set up for the long haul, and how they can pay the least amount of taxes on their investments as possible. That's the theme, and we will try to meet with every single client and review their portfolios from that standpoint."

Armstrong's approach allows him to focus on one major issue at a time. Of course, if there are other major factors to consider, he would not limit the discussion to taxes. This approach allows the clients to bring their CPAs to one meeting and their attorneys to another, instead of having everyone at every meeting. Attending the meeting with other professionals involved in your financial life is important.

---

1. It is possible to have different risk tolerances for different goals. For example, a portions of your assets may be allocated for children's education, which is 15 years in the future. That portion of the portfolio can probably handle more risk than the portions devoted to next year's retirement.

HUDOCK ON INTEGRITY

"*Integrity* is an obvious and vital part of the development of a successful practice. The commitment to do what is right for the client, sometimes at the expense of profitability, is the necessary foundation for the kind of trust that brings about referrals from the best clients—those we want to "clone." No matter which team member a client contacts, the message, the mission and the response should be the same.

We believe that no practice can survive, let alone grow and prosper, without strong *integrity*. We are not a non-profit, and we are entitled to make a living for the value we provide, but, while greed may be a large factor in what drives the markets, it cannot be a factor in what builds a viable financial services firm. We adhere to the philosophy that in doing the right thing that is in the very best interest of our clients at all times, profitability will take care of itself via client satisfaction and referrals."

Barbara B. Hudock
Hudock Moyer Financial Advisors, LLC

CHAPTER **9**

Miscommunications, Mistakes and Misalignments

"I know you understand what you think I said, but I'm not so sure that what you heard is what I meant."

This saying may be written in jest, but the reality is, miscommunication can prove disastrous in financial situations. Miscommunication problems are not always easy to identify, but there are a number of signs you and your advisor can be on the lookout for, as well as a number of useful remedies.

This chapter discusses some "red flags" that can signal trouble or incompatibility between you and an advisor.

Different Meanings and Interpretations

You've now learned how to formulate your investment objectives and how to make sure, during the initial meetings, that you and your advisor have a clear understanding of your long-term needs and objectives. You and your advisor must be in agreement on definitions for such "fuzzy terms" as "good service," "adequate retirement income," and "long-term growth." Being on the same wave-length allows you both to create reasonable, mutually acceptable performance measurement standards, which tell you when you are on or off your financial track. If either of you have unrealistic expectations, then you need to resolve them or agree to part company.

Red Flags from the Investor's Perspective

Caution: Small problems that occur early on could be an indication of bigger problems later. Small problems by an advisor can include: incorrectly spelling your name and not taking the time to fix it, not returning a telephone call or e-mail request within 24 hours, not sending out materials on a timely basis, and not keeping good notes.

James Harris III says a series of small errors should be a red flag when working with financial advisors. If an advisor is not doing the following, you may have cause for concern:

- Are they following through on things they said they were going to do, even simple things (i.e., mailing paperwork to you)? They should "do what they say, say what they do."

- Are they giving you a straightforward, fair answer, or do they beat around the bush?

- Do they communicate with you frequently? If you are not getting a phone call from your advisor at least once a quarter, it could be a problem. (Harris says he talks to his clients an average of once a month.)

- Have the ground rules and processes they follow been laid out? For example: At the first meeting, did the advisor explain what he/she does and the management process that he/she uses?

These are often indications of simple mistakes that can be quickly fixed. But, if the problem is not resolved after one or two attempts to fix it, then you and your advisor must communicate more directly.

A Proactive System

To make sure that nothing slips through the cracks, Barbara B. Hudock,managing principal and member of the investment committee of Hudock Moyer Financial Advisors of Wachovia Securities (Williamsport, PA), has developed a proactive system. She sends out a questionnaire that says, "You are very valuable to us and we want to keep the lines of communication open. Enclosed is a form that gives you the opportunity to voice a compliment about any of our staff members, a concern, a challenge, or an idea." Hudock says, "By sending this out, it let's them know that we care and are listening."

Perhaps the biggest red flag is when an advisor doesn't attempt to periodically update your profile. After all, if your needs have shifted for whatever reason, then adaptations must be made to your plan. While it is your responsibility to alert the advisor, it is also his/her responsibility to regularly check with you.

With more than 20 years of experience in providing invetment management services, Donald R. Parker suggests you may have a problem if you haven't heard from your advisor in six months. "I don't care if you only have $5,000 with him/her or $5 million. It is incumbent upon the advisors to maintain that touch with the client."

George Connell Jr. makes sure he and his clients are "in-tune" with each other and that he knows where he fits into the client's entire picture. He suggests, "If your advisor doesn't seem to be 'in-tune' with you, don't be afraid to ask questions." Following are sample questions Connell suggests investors ask if they don't feel there is a complete understanding of their situation:

1. What role do you feel you are playing in our overall account?

2. Will you alter your investment strategy given our circumstances?

Connell is also very meticulous in his note-taking. He keeps a detailed log of all conversations with clients. He explains, "We always keep a diary that allows us to keep track of the last time we met with the client and what we determined then to be important agenda items for the future. When we call to set an appointment, we remind the client of important points that need to be discussed at the next meeting. We want the agenda to be items that our clients feel are important and therefore everyone comes away feeling the time was well spent."

Harris is also meticulous in his note-taking. He explains, "They include information about asset allocation, goals on rebalancing, how often we want to rebalance, and what we look for in money managers. I use these notes on an on-going basis as a guideline."

Another red flag is when an advisor fails to provide ongoing education (as described in Chapter 19).

Red Flags From the Advisor's Perspective

Red flags go both ways. Advisors must be sensitive to potential changes in client attitude, commitment, and responses. Three advisors provide insights into this.

One advisor mentioned he turned down a $2 million account because of a personality conflict and his fear that the prospective clients had a substance-abuse problem. "It was a fairly complex situation that involved some guardianship issues and I could tell, based on the two conversations with the clients, that I wouldn't be comfortable working with them," he says.

Thomas Curran adds to the list of common red flags. "We are always on guard when a client wants to trade frequently or attempts to time the market since this works against our investment discipline. We are concerned when we present an investor with a long-term strategy and there is an unwillingness or inability to adhere to the plan. Excessive questioning or the reverse, an unwillingness to communicate, also raises questions as to whether the relationship is solid."

Frederick Dawson comments: "Over the years I have found that if someone asks me to reduce my fee, it's a red flag. I don't want them for a client. If someone asks me to reduce my fee, I will say, 'Sure, which part of my services don't you want?'"

If you, or your advisor, feel that there is a "misalignment" of purposes, that is, unrealistic expectations have crept into the equation, then you both need to assess what is going on and communicate with each other. Most of the time, the issue or concern is simple and can be quickly resolved. Allowing any type of dissatisfaction to fester does a disservice to everyone.

When exploring any dissatisfaction, Curran says he asks clients what exactly they are hiring his team to do. He continues, "We then describe the value we have added and justify our fee. We want to know if their unhappiness is with our level of service or performance, or is it because of the market in general."

Jeffrey B. Thomas, Raymond James Financial Services, shares this client story:

"I was having a conversation with a client one morning and was informed that he had just received a severance package. He and his wife had both quit working, were selling their house in Texas and moving to Arkansas. These kinds of decisions change their financial picture significantly. Now we're talking about how much cash we need to raise for a down payment on the new house. How much cash will they get out of their old house? What kind of cash flow, or cash reserves do they need to get them through the transition period? We hadn't talked about these possibilities two years ago, but now it is in the mix. That's the dynamics of people's lives. You have to have flexibility along the way and plan accordingly. That's why it is so important to have good communication with the financial consultant, and make them aware of any changes that occur."

In Conclusion

Miscommunications, mistakes, and misalignments can usually be re-solved quickly if they are addressed early. However, if left unaddressed they can fester and potentially become much larger issues.

DAWSON ON INTEGRITY

"We are compelled to do the best for our clients. We consider ourselves to be CLIENT focused here. We have no quotas; we get no financial incentives or disincentives to recommend one financial product over another. We've never had a formal complaint filed against us. Our compliant file is, and hopefully will remain, empty.

My ChFC and CLU designations mandate that I must do for my clients what I would do for myself if I were in the same financial situation as them. I've lost very few clients over the last 24 years. I think that speaks volumes."

Frederick J. Dawson, ChFC, CLU
Bassett, Brosius & Dawson, Inc.

CHAPTER 10

PROCESS: **Execute**
- To do or carry out fully.
- To put in force.

PROCESS: **Evaluate**
- To appraise or determine the value of.

Execute and Evaluate

I mplementing a financial plan and checking the results are other important components of the PROCESS.

Evaluation of the Initial Plan

Unless you are a highly trained advisor yourself, it would be difficult to fully evaluate a proposed plan of action. Yet, you can feel satisfied with the plan based on how your advisor understands your needs, is able to put them into writing, and describes the "logic" of the plan or strategy. Of course, other professionals you employ may have additional questions to ask the advisor and you may even want a second opinion. Still, at this point, an evaluation of your financial plan is, by necessity, somewhat subjective.

Evaluation of the Results

Once the financial plan has been operating for a while, previously established measurable goals can be objectively evaluated. Is your plan on track? What is the specific performance of your portfolio? How is it doing relative to certain benchmarks? You and the advisor should be evaluating the portfolio based on whether it is behaving within the parameters established at the beginning.

Despite a thorough selection process, there will be times

when the benchmarks of a particular manager underperform. As described more fully in Chapters 15 and 16, it is important to give managers a full-market cycle when measuring performance. However, it is equally important to carefully monitor underperforming managers and, if warranted, replace that manager earlier rather than later. But, keep in mind that the advisor is looking at the big picture and although he/she might make mistakes from time to time, like placing money with a certain money manager who underperforms their respective benchmarks, a good advisor will be quick to recognize and address the issues and work through it. The problem could easily have been that another firm bought the manager and they realigned their research resources. Was it a mistake to hire that manager? No. However, it would be a mistake to continue to maintain that manager knowing they shifted.

Monitoring the Professional Money Manager

How do advisors monitor portfolio performance? They have a host of sophisticated tools that allow them to determine where and how managers add value. The reason advisors must give money managers a full-market cycle before judging performance is that there is no "best" approach to the market. There are a series of overlapping, yet non-simultaneous, cycles that actually drive the investment markets based upon numerous domestic and international economic factors.

Despite all of the historical evidence and logic to the contrary, it is here that many investors lose perspective because of unreasonable, unattainable expectations. Many of the advisors quoted in this book reference the bull market of the 1990s as an example of when investors formed unrealistic expectations. Throughout history, in the vast majority of bull-market cycles there comes a point at which an investor's enthusiasm and exuberance overshadows logic and discipline. They think: "Everybody's making money," "There's no where to go but up!" "Today's highs are tomorrow's lows," and, "This is a new economy, the old rules don't apply." Somewhere near the market peak, over-enthusiasm and unrealistic expectations reach their highest pitch. At this point (and it's polar opposite) is when many investors want to shift gears by changing to an investment strategy that will make fast, easy money. But it doesn't work that way.

Frederick Dawson had to fire a money manager based on several reasons: The manager's performance was poor relative to his peer group and relative to his anticipated benchmark, and there had been a management change at the company. He explains, "When I saw their standard deviation was excessive relative to their returns I said to my clients 'You don't need this amount of risk, even though you are making money.' Sometimes my clients have a hard time understanding my suggestions. 'Why are you firing this guy? He's making money. He's doing better than some of the others.' We talk about the risk adjusted returns. I really try to hold on to my discipline. I find in those times when I weaken, I usually regret it. I try to instill in my clients a sense of discipline too."

Managing Expectations

One of the most difficult jobs of an advisor is managing investor expectations and getting them to do the right thing. This strategy has two

Two case studies, provided by Donald R. Parker, founder, Gryphon Valuation Consultants, illustrate the consequences of not following an investment discipline. "It's difficult," he says, "to bring an institutional mindset to individual investors because of the emotions involved."

"I took on two clients at the same time about a year ago. In my professional opinion and through the development of an Investment Policy Statement (IPS) for each, I determined, and they agreed, that their assets needed to be managed in the same way: preserve and protect while providing for a hedge against inflation. Neither client had a current need for the use of their assets for income. Both had a bad habit of checking the value of their portfolios daily when possible. From the outset, the equity portion (25%) of their portfolios performed poorly (in line with the appropriate benchmarks, but still were loosing money).

I lost one client after two months. I estimate that his inability to remove emotion from the equation and his insistence on focusing on the short-term gain cost him over half of what his portfolio would be worth today both because he didn't stick with the plan—a plan that he signed off on—and because of what he did with his assets after firing me—he went to all cash.

The other client was as equally focused on the short-term and as equally emotionally persuaded by fluctuations in value. For what ever reason, and for all the plight he caused himself and me, he decided to stay the course. Today, because of his equity allocation, his portfolio is worth 20% more than its initial value, even though at one point it was worth 20% less.

Here's the kicker, though: He still curses me for the anguish he caused himself by not being able to remove emotion from the equation and his inability to focus on long-term goals. Conversely, the client that fired me apologizes to me every time I see him. What he's really doing is asking for forgiveness for not being able to see the long-term vision in the plan that we jointly developed. If the two people in these two situations were boards of trustees instead of individuals, I would be receiving accolades-a-million for my ability to steer their financial ships through the storms of volatility and return to shore with my booty in tact and then some.

points of focus: 1) staying the course with the investment strategy that was initially embarked upon, and 2) if the investor had been hurt in a bad market, convincing him/her to abandon the old strategy and adopt one that would help them attain their financial objectives.

Next Step - Execution

"Sometimes, ya just gotta do it."

Clients, in most situations, can easily see the logic of the advisor's plan of action and are willing to immediately implement the suggestions. However, some clients avoid executing the plan of action for a host of reasons, including:

- *Fear of change.* Most adults are "change-phobic." The thought of changing jobs, relationships, residences, etc., is extremely disquieting to them. They get a knot in the pit of their stomachs. But not making a decision is, in fact, making a decision.

- *Procrastination.* (As an aside: The simplest cure for procrastination is to postpone procrastinating.) Ira Rapaport notes, "With tax returns, people understand they have a deadline. They know they have to file their returns and pay their tax liabilities by April 15. Unfortunately, people don't also make estate planning a priority. They don't want to focus on, 'What will happen if I die?' It's the job of a trusted advisor to make sure that it is taken care of."

- *Paralysis by analysis*. People who explore and evaluate different alternatives to an extreme often end up doing nothing. This "need to know it all" syndrome paralyzes the decision-making process.

- *"I'm too busy."* Rapaport makes a good point about how some advisors counsel with clients, yet their suggestions never get implemented. He continues, "Because I have a higher level of knowledge about the client and their different disciplines, I can coordinate and make sure things get implemented in a timely fashion. "

- *"Need to talk it over"* or *"Let me think about it"* syndromes. Occasionally, these responses are appropriate. The problem occurs when people get mixed messages by talking to too many people, experts or not. So they talk to a few more people! If an investor needs to "think about it," this usually implies one or more issues or questions have not been discussed. In this case, the investor needs to go to his/her advisor for an answer and then make a decision.

- *Mistrust.* Trust is usually developed after the investor has met with an advisor, checked his/her credentials and references, and become familiar with the advisor's process. If this doesn't happen or there is a breakdown along the way, mistrust occurs.

- *Fear.* Fear takes many forms—fear of making a mistake, of the market going down, etc. You should have an equal or greater fear of "doing nothing."

- *Greed.* This manifests itself through the belief that the market is about to go up or will continue to go up, and the desire to capture additional profits rather than doing the most appropriate thing. Greed causes more portfolio disasters than almost anything other factor.

- *"Tail wagging the dog"* response. One client wouldn't take a profit because he would have to pay taxes on his huge capital gains. Instead, he watched his portfolio deteriorate to less than 10 percent of its original value.

- *Getting in slowly.* Brent Bentrim provides this analogy: "If you go to the doctor and something is wrong with you, and he calls back and says you've got an aggressive cancer and you need chemotherapy, you don't say, 'You know, I've never had cancer before. I think I'll start off with aspirin.'"

In Conclusion

There is a multifaceted evaluation process in which you evaluate the logic of the financial plan, the advisor evaluates the money manager and the performance of the portfolio, and you evaluate yourself to ensure you don't get caught up in the emotions of the market. Once you have seen the logic of the plan, it is your responsibility to yourself, you family and your legacy to implement it.

❖ ❖ ❖

In the investment process it is important to value all of your assets, not just financial vehicles. Since the value of your business, real estate and other tangible and intangible assets may constitute a significant portion of your net worth, it is important they be appropriately valued.

Donald R. Parker, founder of Gryphon Valuation Consultants, identifies and enhances value for business owners. He explains his services, "I will analyze a company's historical financials and apply advanced valuation techniques and methodologies, then in addition, forecast earnings, projections, conduct economic and industry analysis amongst other research. it is a very research-intensive process. I will then overlay the analytical results on top of the research and empirical data to derive a valuation based upon any number of factors."

He says it is also important to understand the complexity of business, such as buy-sell agreements, start-up enterprises, alternative compensation arrangements (stock options, ESOPs, etc.), and mergers and acquisitions to name a few.

CURRAN ON INTEGRITY

"Curran Investment Management of Wachovia Securities is a knowledgeable, results-oriented team of professionals dedicated to meeting its clients' unique needs. We offer our clients a traditional, common-sense approach to successful investing and our commitment to provide the highest level of personal service and attention. We believe in developing and maintaining client relationships based on trust and frequent communication. Our investment process is client-driven and is focused on providing investment management tailored to each client's goals. Our investment management services are exclusively fee-based which eliminates any conflict of interest inherent in commission-based business and aligns our interests with our clients. Our investment process is the foundation for our business and is central to every client relationship. Our goal is to add value."

Thomas Curran, MBA
Curran Investment Management
Wachovia Securities

PROCE**SS**: **Systems**
- Assemblage of objects arranged after some distinct method.
- Whole scheme of created things regarded as forming one complete whole.
- Organization.
- Set of doctrines or principles.

Systems Ensure Success

The watch analogy presented in Chapter 2, which explains how many gears must work together to give you the correct time, is a good way of describing how systems work within systems. When you engage the services of a high-level financial advisor, you engage more than his/her knowledge, experience, dedication, and concern. You also engage an entire system of people, technology, resources and relationships that allow the financial-planning process to occur seamlessly, each and every time. At least, that is way the process is intended to work. In reality, does every single sub-system and procedure work each and every time? Of course not. But, in many cases these high-level advisors have built the operating systems themselves, fine-tuned them over time, and are dedicated to constantly making everything work better. After all, that is one of the ways they differentiate themselves from traditional advisors.

The "gears" within the operating system take many forms—technology, people, processes—some of which have already been reviewed in this book. They include:

- Performance evaluations systems (Also see Chapter 16) through which advisors can monitor the performance of money managers throughout the industry.

- Client-contact systems to ensure that each client is contacted and updates occur on a regularly scheduled basis. High-level advisors don't just call to sell you something.

- Team systems are in place to ensure that a coordinated effort is made on your behalf. Cross-training of personnel is just one example.

- Professional continuing education is pursued by advisors and many of the team members to upgrade their skills and knowledge.

- Integrated computer software may be a part of the process depending on the size of the advisor's firm and the firm's commitment to technology.

- A network of other professionals who may be part of a strategic alliance with the advisor's firm. (To be discussed in Chapter 12.)

All of the above, plus many other systems and processes, go into making a successful financial advisory practice. Some of the main systems are described below in more detail.

According to Stephen Winks[1], editor of *Senior Consultant* on-line publication, "Nobel Prize-winning investment theory is converging with advanced systems technology to empower advisors to deliver an unprecedented level of professional investment and administrative counsel." Investors, as consumers, are interested in their financial advisors adding value in terms specifically meaningful to them. Yet, very few financial advisors can tell their clients the precise rate of return achieved on their assets as an investment portfolio. They cannot determine if the investor is taking 150 percent of the market risk to realize 50 percent of its return. They cannot determine whether the investor's assets are structured in an income and estate tax efficient manner. They cannot estimate the cost structure of the investor's portfolio.

It is important to adopt the appropriate technology and embrace all of the processes involved in offering high-level advice. For those advisors who fail to adopt the process and technology necessary to add value, it is very difficult to compete at the very high end of the market. As human beings we can only think in three dimensions. If we tried to think in the fifth or tenth dimension we cannot phantom 25 or 100 possible interrelated outcomes. Now consider this mind-boggling example. Assume an advisor wants to add value for 500 clients who each *have only one* investment objective of retirement. In order to manage the six investment values of risk, return, tax efficiency, liquidity, cost structure, and time, and using the 10,000 investment options at their disposal, each with 100 description points, the advisor would have to consider a 3 billion dimensional equation with 9 quintillion (18 zeros!) possible interrelated investment outcomes. Clearly today's financial product and service menu has become mind boggling. No one understands it in its entirety, much less can articulate it."

Summarizing Wink's comments, he explains that only with process and technology is it possible for one to manage a massive volume of data so advisors can address and manage the full range of investment and administrative values for each individual investor as required by regulatory mandate. The six financial service investment processes are:

1. Asset Study,

2. Investment Policy Statement,

3. Strategic Asset Allocation,

4. Manager Search and Selection,

5. Performance Monitoring, and

6. Tactical Asset Allocation

The *Asset Study* is the most powerful sales tool available to the advisor. It establishes a reference point on how the investor's assets and liabilities look as an investment portfolio, and from which the financial advisor can measure the value they add. Most investors have no idea how all their assets and liabilities look in investment portfolio, but without this point of reference it is impossible to determine if an investment recommendation improves overall portfolio return, reduces risk, improves tax efficiency, etc.

The asset study establishes 20 to 30 ways the advisor can immediately improve the investor's financial affairs, while establishing instant credibility with any investor - whether an individual or an institution. The investor discovers that there has been no one accountable for helping them achieve their broad range of goals and objectives.

The next step in the process is development of a *Statement of Investment Policy* for the investor. It is the heart and soul of the investment process because it provides a cohesive investment focus, offers a framework for the investor, the advisor, and the money manager to work together. It keeps everyone focused on goals and objectives while it establishes and documents investment strategy. It becomes the "corporate conscious" that governs the client relationship.

Strategic Asset Allocation is the next step. (Although it is technically part of the Investment Strategy, it is so important that it is treated as a separate financial service.) Numerous studies have concluded that about 96 percent of investment returns are determined by the configuration of asset classes in which one invests. Approximately 4 percent of investment performance is attributable to manager selection. Therefore, being in the right configuration of asset classes determines most of the value added. The strategic asset allocation establishes the asset classes and investment management styles in which to invest.

Manager Search and Selection is the next step in the process. The advisor is looking for the best performing manager in each investment management style peer group at a reasonable price.

The next step, *Performance Monitoring,* is where the advisor continues to add value by evolving the investment policy and strategy based on changing market conditions and investor needs. The advisor must continue to educate the client and manage client expectations, while maintaining the discipline necessary for long-term success.

Without doubt, competitors will try to woo the investor. BUT, unless that competitor can understand the risk, tax efficiency, cost structure, and objectives, he/she can't hope to add value.

Tactical Asset Allocation is the final process as the advisor notes which investment styles fall in and out of favor and adjusts accordingly.

---

1. Stephen Winks is the editor of *Senior Consultant* on-line publication and the foremost proponent of the "advice business model." This information was taken from *The Mega Producers: Secrets of Financial Services Superstars to Lead You to the Top* (Dearborn 2003) by Steven Drozdeck

Systems Ensure Success

DeWees on Integrity

"We have always believed that if we do what's in the best interests of the client, everything else will take care of itself...and it has! Our practice is 100 percent referral driven (mostly from clients, and to a lesser extent, other professionals). By educating our clients on what we do and why we do it, we have created a solid base of knowledgeable advocates."

Donald C. DeWees Jr., CIMA, CIS
DeWees Investment Consulting Group

PROCES**S**: **Synchronize**
- To be simultaneous.
- To cause to occur at the same time.
- Concurrence of events.

A Synchronized
Team Effort

Working with multiple advisors without having an overall, guiding plan is a major problem for many investors. The insurance agent knows the insurance side of the client. The stockbroker usually only knows portions of the investment portfolio. Private bankers know some things but not others. The same applies to the legal and accounting professionals in a client's life – they don't necessarily know the whole picture. Too many people use this patchwork approach to financial planning and then wonder why they don't attain their goals and objectives.

There are investors who like to "keep their cards close to their chest" so that they are the only ones who know the complete picture. This is not necessarily because they are private people– although some are—but because they don't want to constantly hear the "bring-it-all-under-one-roof" sales pitch from each of their commissioned advisors. Given the complexity of today's world, it would be hard to imagine one person so brilliant that he could keep all of your financial information, interrelationships and permutations in his head.

Industry surveys by the New York Stock Exchange and the Securities Industry Association, to name only two, have repeatedly demonstrated that affluent investors employ multiple (traditional) financial advisors and institutions, with each one receiving only a portion of that investor's overall assets. One of the reason for this may be that commission-based brokers try to gather all of the investor's assets in one location to generate more revenue. Another reason is they rarely get a comprehensive picture of their client's financial picture; hence, can, at best, only provide partial solutions. This is in stark contrast to the approach taken by high-level financial advisors. Their fee is based on the size and complexity of the account, not on what is bought or sold. Repeating an important point from earlier chapters, high-level advisors have made a business decision to always sit on the same side of the table as their clients.

A Complete Team

If an investor already has a team of competent financial and legal advisors, then those people should be brought into the process. If the client doesn't have an attorney who specializes in estates, for example, the financial advisor may recommend one. Sometimes the estate attorney may be a member of the advisor's internal team or, in other cases, an outside strategic-alliance partner. A strategic-alliance partnership is a relationship between two or more professionals or firms that provide supplementary professional services to the advisor. Accountants and attorneys with specialized knowledge are the most common examples. Real estate, business valuation services, insurance professionals, loan specialists, and trust administrators are a sampling of other counselors who may be brought in for specific client needs and situations. The point is, the high-level financial advisor will have a network of high-level professionals to draw upon.

High-level advisors and their teams can often comment on, or help evaluate, the documents prepared by other professionals. Jacques Abrams, for example, says he has a number of clients who had attorneys help them in the area of estate planning, when in reality the attorneys were not experts in this area. Many times the documents they provide leave "something to be desired," he says. The problem could be that the "cookie cutter" estate plan hasn't been customized to meet the specific needs or desires of the client. Abrams comments, "I feel it is my responsibility to bring, with the client's permission, these 'issues' to the attorney's attention so that they can be resolved."

Barbara Hudock tells us, "Usually, when the client is scheduling to meet with the attorney, my business partner or I will be part of the meeting, because I can help demystify the legal process for the client, and also make sure the attorney understands what the client wants to do. Both sides tend to appreciate us doing that. They feel that everyone is working together for their client's best interest."

Ira Rapaport also likes to work with his client's other professional advisors. "I encourage it," he says. "I think it is great to have a strategic partnership with clients where I'm driving the bus, and we have the attorney, CPA, insurance agents, and private banker on board. The idea is to get everyone working toward the same goals and to provide the best ideas in an open forum for communication. A good example would be the relationship with their CPA. We would discuss with them how the client's investments have done throughout the year. Then we'll decide: Do we want to harvest losses? Do we want to make a charitable gift? How can we reduce the tax liability?"

As Lisa T. Clifford, associate vice president of Curran Investment Management (Albany, NY) says, "We encourage the client to bring his other advisors into our relationship."

Every advisor in this book agrees with, and actively encourages, this team approach. Some advisors regularly meet with other professionals by sponsoring educational seminars or they meet privately with a client's professional advisors to provide updates. Thomas Curran indicates that he regularly meets with clients' attorneys and CPAs to update them. He'll then provide them with copies of correspondence, with the client's permission. He goes a step further and writes a quarterly newsletter for such professionals, updating them on different aspects of the investment process.

Internal Teams

Many high-level advisors also have their own internal teams comprised of CFPs®, CFAs®, CLUs, CIMAs, JDs, and other professional designations. (These designations are de-

> **Barbara B. Hudock, managing principal and member of the Investment Committee of HMFA** tells us, "If I think one attorney has a personality that will fit with the clients, we'll make that recommendation, but will give them several choices as well. If they need the expertise of an attorney who charges $350 an hour, then we'll tell them that. If I think they have basic estate planning issues, I'll tell them. Clients really appreciate that. In one case I called one attorney and told her about the situation, asked for her advice and she said, 'It's over my head. You need to talk to one of my colleagues about this.' The client didn't object to the $350 an hour because she knew she needed the expertise. I have never had a client who didn't welcome me calling their accountant or attorney if I felt it would be beneficial to them or if I needed more information about their situation in order to make a recommendation for them."

scribed in Chapter 17.)

Adam Westphalen realizes that one person just can't do it all. His comment on teamwork and communication between all professionals summarizes the need to include everyone in the process. "We have specific attorneys and accounting capabilities in-house. We talk to our attorneys on numerous occasions to get their input. If someone already has a relationship, we will include him or her in the discussions, whether they come to our office, or we go to the attorney's office. The key components to our efforts are to coordinate the communication between them and our client. If the client's various advisors – be it the attorneys, CPAs, or other financial professionals – don't communicate, it's a recipe for disaster. If they don't already have relationships with other advisors, than we can certainly help them with that."

Understanding Personal Capabilities

Abrams, as well as many of the other high-level advisors, specializes in a particular market niche so he is cognizant of what he can and cannot do for a client. The adage that "A wise man knows what he doesn't know" applies here. As Abrams explains, "When you deal with very high-net-worth clients, the issues are complex in regard to the various trusts to be considered, e.g., charitable remainder trusts, grantor trusts, etc. Transferring family values is particularly important. I like to deal with clients where the issues are sufficiently complex so as to obviate straightforward, 'cookie cutter' solutions. Nevertheless, I'm realistic and recognize that when a family has a net worth of $10 million to $20 million, I don't have the personal skill set to adequately provide the range of services such a situation requires.

"When appropriate, I refer them to organizations better suited to meet their needs. What frustrates me at times is the awareness that some organizations catering to the needs of the very wealthy may, at the same time, place a high level of emphasis on maximizing remuneration via the fees they charge. While I realize that it may be naïve, I am a strong believer that when you strive to do the very best for your clients, the financial component for the provider of these services will, in most situations, work out."

In conclusion, it is important to realize that teamwork makes a major difference in helping you achieve your goals. If you have a team of high-level professionals behind you, you maximize your probability of financial success in a growingly complex world.

❖ ❖ ❖

A Synchronized Team Effort

BENTRIM ON INTEGRITY

" I think *integrity* really revolves around the adult definition of honesty. As a child we are taught not to lie, that honesty is only a reactive trait. My opinion is that honesty is, in reality, a proactive measure. It is fully disclosing all conflicts and fees to clients. It is being a good steward of their wealth and your own. *Integrity* incorporates speaking up and pointing out issues that may not be of comfort to yourself or the client. It is active and ongoing."

Brent E. Bentrim, CFM
Carolopolis Family Wealth Management

CHAPTER 13

Fiduciary Responsibility

A ccording to *Barron's Dictionary of Finance and Investment Terms*, a fiduciary is "a person, company, or association holding assets in trust for a beneficiary. The fiduciary is charged with the responsibility of investing the money wisely for the beneficiary's benefit."

The definitions of fiduciary and the laws of fiduciary responsibility vary from state to state, but the consensus of the advisors in this book is that, regardless of the legal definition, if a person or institution relies upon you for advice, then you are a fiduciary. Additionally, while some financial firms make the legal argument that providing advice to clients is only incidental to providing trade execution, most industry professions believe that financial advisors should hold themselves to a higher standard. Whether an advisor holds the title of Investment Advisor, Registered Investment Advisor, Account Executive, Financial Advisor, Financial Consultant or Investment Planner, the name implies that he or she has a certain level of knowledge that makes him/her capable of helping investors select appropriate financial products or strategies. While the client makes the final investment decision, it is often strongly influenced by, or totally dependent on, the recommendation(s) make by the advisor.

Most of the advisors interviewed for this book, as well as high-level advisors everywhere, would generally agree in principle with the following statements made by George Connell Jr. and Donald DeWees Jr.

> Connell: "Advisors take on a fiduciary role in the course of contributing toward a client's future financial success."

> DeWees: "I have a 100 percent obligation in all three areas of the process. Every advisor does, whether they admit it or not. At the brokerage firms under the broker-dealer, they feel they're insulated somewhat, but in my opinion they are not. Anyone who is giving comprehensive investment advice is a fiduciary whether they acknowledge it or not."

The best way to precisely define the fiduciary responsibility of an advisor would be to draft it into law. Until then, you must rely on an advisor exercising moral responsibility and personal ethics. Chapter 17 discusses some industry designations and provides web addresses to the Code of Ethics or Standards that each person receiving the designation must subscribe to.

Things to Know if You are a Fiduciary

Some people reading this book may be on a board of directors, an investment committee, or an oversight committee of a company or charitable institution. Depending on the type of company or committee you are associated with and the laws that apply to that group, you may have fiduciary responsibility and could be held accountable for the appropriateness of the investments under your care. Also, lack of financial knowledge may not be a viable legal defense. If you hold this type of position, be sure to check with your attorney for legal liability.

The following federal and state standards deal with key financial responsibility issues.

- Uniform Management of Institutional Funds Act (UMIFA) for Endowments and Foundations,
- Uniform Management of Public Employee Retirement System Act (UMPERS also known as MPERS) for Public Funds,
- Employee Retirement Income Security Act (ERISA) for Defined Benefit, Contribution and Profit Sharing Plans,
- Uniform Trust Code for trusts,
- Uniform Prudent Investors Act (UPIA) for all individual investors

(Uniform state laws passed in 39 states – as of this writing.)

In addition, organizations within the financial services industry have laid out non-regulatory standards that advisors are strongly encouraged to follow. For example, The Foundation for Fiduciary Studies has created Uniform Fiduciary Standards of Care. (See Chapter 17.) Very specific standards for dealing with the high-net-worth market are currently being drafted.

David Bromelkamp explains, "When talking about fiduciary responsibilities, a lot of people don't know that each state has laws regarding fiduciary obligations. One of the most common misunderstandings occurs when an individual establishes a private foundation. When someone puts money into a private foundation, the money is gifted to a charitable entity (the private foundation) and it is no longer the donor's money. Instead, it becomes property of the charity and a fiduciary relationship is created between the board members of the private foundation and the charitable beneficiaries of the foundation. This fiduciary relationship is regulated at the state level by the state attorney general who has the responsibility to oversee all of the tax-exempt charitable organizations in that particular state. The donors to the private foundation sometimes think it's still their own personal money."

Bromelkamp has just taken the Accredited Investment Fiduciary Auditor (AIFA) course that was developed by Don Trone and the Center for Fiduciary Studies. The recently published *Prudent Investment Practices: A Handbook for Investment Fiduciaries* out-

David Bromeklamp, senior vice president of RBC Dain Rauscher Senior Consulting Group, provides insight into the needs and responsibilities of fiduciaries.

"We work with fiduciary investors in the "middle-market" which we classify as portfolios from $1 million to $100 million. Fiduciary investors would include foundations, endowments, retirement plan trustees and the trustees of private and charitable trusts. Many of the volunteer boards of nonprofit organizations and foundations & endowments don't fully understand the standards which apply to them and therefore do not know how to invest their portfolios in compliance with the existing fiduciary investment laws that apply to their organizations – it's not that they're not good people – it's just that nobody has ever given them guidance on how to do it. Our team's goal during the next 5-10 years to educate fiduciary investors about how to do it the right way. We do this mostly through educational workshops for clients as well as teaching Continuing Education courses to CPAs and attorneys. I do a lot of public speaking. We believe that we can help improve the investment practices of fiduciaries by educating their advisors – their CPAs and their attorneys."

lines 27 practices that define a prudent investment process for fiduciaries. Bromelkamp says understanding the discipline of the fiduciary investment process is helpful to any individual investor. He says, "We manage investment portfolios the same way for affluent individuals as we do for our fiduciary clients. Same investment managers, same asset allocation and rebalancing, same cost. There is no major difference between managing a portfolio for an individual investor and a fiduciary investor, except that individuals have tax-related issues such as, estate taxes, income taxes, college planning, and retirement planning. That's why we have a Certified Financial Planner™ (CFP®) on our team."

Foundation Consultants

Matthew Potter has become a consultant to the foundations and endowments market because he found it rewarding to work with other trustees or plan sponsors. He says, "I recently was invited to attend a conference sponsored by the Institute for Fiduciary Education. There were only 100 people attending, one-third of us were trustees or plan sponsors, representing $520 billion worth of assets. Because I've enjoyed it so much, I've started to reach out more to foundations and endowments to provide consulting services.

Potter serves on a retirement board that manages $4.5 billion for 50,000 members. "As the chairman of the board, I get to work with 10 other board members who are all very conscientious about what they're doing. I get to work with some very bright people in the consulting business. It is terribly exciting," he says.

Potter says he considers himself fortunate to have so many competent people surrounding him in the consulting business. Other advisors and industry experts say this is not always the case. Too often, these sources have said, the trustees of certain foundations and endowments abdicate their investment responsibility and turn over some or all of the money to a buddy who says he can pick stocks and bonds. Anyone who holds a position of responsibility with a foundation (or pension, or trust, etc.) should have advisors with strong credentials, a proven track record, and high ethical standards.

A Stewardship

In conclusion, you, the investor, should expect your advisor to think of himself/herself as a steward of your money or a fiduciary. Whether you are responsible for your own money or that of a company, pick an advisor who has a strong sense of responsibility for your welfare.

WESTPHALEN ON INTEGRITY

" The definition of integrity includes the words 'honesty' and 'uprightness of character.' I don't think I've ever encountered a financial advisor who didn't include the word honesty in his/her mission statement or value proposition. The challenge for the individual investor is knowing when to trust an advisor and how to determine if they are truly 'honest.'

Integrity creates a requirement for advisors to uphold high standards of professionalism. At Vista, we have created an environment that demonstrates to potential and existing clients that we operate in an objective, comprehensive and conflict-free manner.

Our high degree of *integrity* is exhibited through full disclosure of fees, expenses and occasionally, where applicable, commissions. This is the *only* way we can demonstrate *integrity*."

Adam Westphalen, CIMA, CFP®, CPTx
Vista Financial Strategies

CHAPTER 14

Managing Expectations:
Historical Perspectives

Asset allocation (allocating your portfolio holdings among various asset class such as stocks, bonds and cash) accounts for 91.5 percent of a portfolio's performance. That revelation was revealed in "Determinations of Portfolio Performance II: An Update," a landmark study by Brinson, Singer, and Beebower, which appeared in the *Financial Analyst Journal*, May-June 1991. The study provided new insights for investors and investment professionals alike. It further showed that only 4.6 percent of the entire portfolio return was due to security selection, 2.1 percent from market timing, and 1.8 percent from other factors.

Subsequent studies have provided similar results and repeatedly show that time in the market (that is, investing for the long-term) is another key ingredient for success. Asset allocation plus long-term investing maximizes your probability for success.

James Whiddon shares this exercise: Take any long-term (30 or more years) graph of the stock market and then miniaturize yourself and imagine that you are standing at miscellaneous points on the chart looking backward over the previous 10 and 20 years. You'll see that you are always looking down the hill; that is, the value of the market was quite a bit less than it is from where you are standing.

Conversely, if you had a crystal ball at any point in time between 1940 and 1990 and were able to see the dramatic rise in the value of the markets between then and now, wouldn't you want to invest immediately?

Getting to the Top

Investing is like taking a car ride to the top of a mountain. You set a goal to get to the top. You know that the drive will lead you over occasional flat and downhill portions of roadway – but they are immaterial as long as you are generally going up.

As Whiddon explains, "Fluctuations are normal; they are to be expected. Temporary declines lead to further gains that become permanent gains. Things go in cycles. It's normal, it's expected, it's even desired. Those temporary declines are the only things that lead to permanent gains."

Similarly, on average if you move three steps forward and one step back, what difference does the one step back make if you have still a high probability of attaining your goal? None, especially if the probability of reaching it is even lower if you insist on *always* going forward. The same is true for investments. Those who "time the market" to get in at the beginning of bull markets and try to get out during bear markets (hoping to always go up) usually do poorly in comparison to those who buy and hold for the long term.

Why, then, is it that so many investors insist on the low-probability strategy? Stock market history repeatedly demonstrates that crowd euphoria (unrealistic expectations) is greatest near the peak of a bull market. While the peaking stage of a bull market may last for months, this stage usually represents only 10 percent to 15 percent of the rise, with 85 percent to 90 percent of the bull market move having already been realized. It is usually at these times that investment publications and newsletters are printing headlines like, "Today's highs are tomorrow's lows," "We're in a new economy," "How high is up?" "We've only just begun," and "Happy days are here again." In response to this euphoria, ask yourself, "If everybody is buying, who is selling?" The answer usually is: the professionals.

The next question to ask yourself is: "Do I want to invest like a professional (like Warren Buffett) or an amateur?" If you want to invest like a professional, then you must have the required knowledge, technical abilities, and discipline to do the job – or hire somebody who does. If you hire somebody, then make sure you give him/her the authority and the time to do an effective job.

Historical Perspectives and Future Inferences

"Those who do not study the past are doomed to repeat its errors."

Many people mentally project the continuation of a trend – the market will continue to go up, inflation will remain high/low/stable, etc. Another assumption has been that once you retire, your income is taxed at a lower marginal rate. (See case study.)

Discipline

James Whiddon says that if you have enough money to meet your goals and beyond, you may be taking unnecessary risks by trying to beat the market. On the other hand, some people need additional risk. The key is for clients to have a plan, or a road map, to guide their actions rather than steering with their emotions.

Whiddon says that most of his clients appreciate facts, figures, and historical data. "Our clients include engineers and accountants, attorneys, physicians, and dentists. Whatever their backgrounds, there is a similar thread running through their thinking patterns. They are sequential thinkers,

Reginald A.T. Armstrong, president, Armstrong Wealth Management Group, points out that tax rates are also subject to very wide fluctuation. He says, "Taxes can be more devastating than people realize. Many don't realize that despite the fact that income tax came into being in 1913 and now we are enjoying a high marginal tax bracket of 35%, in 1944-45, the highest marginal tax bracket was 94%. The lowest was 23%. One of the things people don't realize is there are two truths about taxation, the treasury always takes in more money one year compared to a previous year. The other truth is, the tax brackets go hand-in-hand with the health of the economy. For example, in the roaring 20s we had a great economy with very low tax brackets. Then we ended up having the great depression, a quarter of Americans out of work. The top marginal tax rate shot up from 25% to 63% in one year—1932. During the 40s, with the World War going on, it went even higher. In the 50s, with the Korean War and under Eisenhower the rates didn't come down. The highest tax brackets in the 50s were over 89%. In the 60s we finally got a reduction of rates, a good economy. In the 70s under Nixon, Ford and Carter, we had stagflation. We didn't get much movement on rates. And when Reagan came in office in 1981 the highest marginal tax bracket was 70%. Then, finally, we got a reduction to 28%. Since then the top bracket has been between 28% and 40%. Therefore, if you are 60, there is no guarantee that over the next 30 years you will enjoy lower tax brackets. We look at taxation at a very long-term perspective."

they're scientific. We use a lot of data to show them what markets have actually done, and to establish that markets in every asset class or sector go in cycles, and that the fundamental problem of most investors is

When asked about historical perspectives and portfolio management, **Thomas Curran, director of investments and Certified Portfolio Manager, Curran Invesment Management of Wachovia,** says, "We have a strict investment discipline we adhere to that helps ensure the long-term strategy is implemented and helps remain on track. We educate our clients by showing them what our audited performance has been. We also share with them the historical rates of return for different asset classes, keeping in mind that past performance does not indicate future performance."

In the August 2003 issue of *Curran Views*, a publication that Curran sends to all of his clients, he writes: "As you know my definition of financial security is based on long-term considerations. Consider the words of Benjamin Graham, the famous mentor of Warren Buffett:

'A serious investor is not likely to believe that the day-to-day or even month-to-month fluctuations of the stock market make him richer or poorer.'

Unfortunately, too many people believe their long-term financial security is impacted by short-term fluctuations in the stock markets. To avoid the possibility of market losses, many trade in and out of the market believing that they are apparently endowed with 'super-human' abilities that enable them to avoid and limit market losses. Trading and timing markets over the short-term often jeopardizes the very goal that is being pursued – long-term financial security.

It is very interesting to me that in spite of all the evidence that supports long-term investing, the following research tells us that investors are falling short of realizing their expected "returns.

"Dalbar, one of the nation's leading financial services research firms, studied investor returns from 1984 through December 2000. They reported the following, which illustrates the benefit of buy-and-hold strategies:

- *The average fixed-income investor realized an annualized return of 6.08 percent, compared to 11.83 percent for the long-term Government Bond Index;*

- *The average equity-fund investor realized an annualized return of 5.32 percent, compared to 16.29 percent for the S&P 500 Index; and,*

- *The average money-market fund investor realized an annualized return of 2.29 percent, compared to 4.82 percent for Treasury Bills and 3.23 percent for inflation. Money-market fund investors lose money after inflation.*[1]

As I mentioned on numerous occasions in previous editions of *Curran Views*, there seems to be the ever-present danger that investors migrate to the asset class that has performed best, rather than buy the asset class that has performed worst. Sometimes we refer to the phenomenon as 'buy high, sell low.'"

to chase returns. As Confucius once said, 'He who chases two rabbits catches neither.' That's the way people are about their investment expectations. We live in such a media-rich world where we hear so much about top-performing stocks or funds. It's easy for investors to become frustrated with their own progress based on the results of the very best investment of the day. Our job, in terms of managing expectations, is to give them perspective. If we can provide them with perspective of what the markets have done and what they should expect from the markets in the future, regardless of what has happened in the last three to six years, then we've done our jobs."

George Connell Jr. emphasizes the need to allow for a full-market cycle to evaluate the performance of money managers – a time discipline. He says, "Time is a key element in that managers require time in order to produce results typical for that management style over a full-market cycle. It is not unusual to see a client get frustrated with interim performance, but when the client wants to make wholesale changes a few quarters into their relationship with a manager, it is important to revisit the client's expectations."

He continues, "To ensure that the client and I are on the same page, I'll ask about their expectations for future returns in relation to the risks they are willing to take to achieve those returns."

In Conclusion

If your portfolio is well-diversified and you follow the right process and give it time, then your portfolio should weather most storms. As David Bromelkamp says, "We've weathered the recent bear market primarily because our investment advice is process-oriented and based on diversification to minimize investment risk. We believe that our clients suffered less volatility over the past few years because they were adequately diversified."

It's important to have a sense of historical perspective, remembering that those who do not study the past are doomed to repeat its errors. It can be difficult to maintain long-term objectivity, particularly when the market looks bleak, yet that is the precisely what you must do to achieve long-term success.

---

1. Dalbar study, published 6/21/01

DeArantes-Oliveira
on Integrity

"*Integrity* must be the beginning and end point of any practice. As the beginning, it must be the point from which all products and services are designed. The mission statement, the strategic business units, marketing and business plan, the personnel and management—all must be formed from a perspective of integrity: the *client* is at the center of our business model and of our universe.

At the end point, *integrity* must be the reason for conducting this business and executing on the business model. At the end of the day, the foremost criterion must be: Did I do the right thing for my clients?

Integrity is defined as responsibility toward the client, toward employees, toward our partner, toward our profession and toward ourselves."

Martim DeArantes-Oliveira, ChFC, CLU
H & S Financial Advisors

CHAPTER 15

Managing Expectations:
Psychology of Investing

S cattered throughout this chapter are numerous Wall Street adages that apply to the psychology of investing, such as: *"Most of us tend to be wrong most of the time, especially when we agree with one another."* This chapter continues the discussion of how to invest, but emphasizes the need to steer clear of decision-making based purely on your emotions or what "everyone else" is doing.

It's easy to get "carried away with the crowd," whether it concerns stock market enthusiasm or despair. Investors are surrounded by advice – from the media, associates at the water cooler, and people at various parties who all seem to be making money. That is why it's important to remember, *"If you hear that 'everyone' is buying, ask who is selling?"* Far too many people get drunk on the excitement of making money in a bull market and start to believe that their superior skills and knowledge (or their stockbroker's) are responsible. Keep in mind that "scientific experiments" of monkeys throwing darts at stock listings in newspapers produce investment returns that are the same as or better than the averages.

A good example of investor overconfidence was experienced during the bull market of the late 90s— many people decided it was "easy" to manage their own investments, until the market started turning downward. Perhaps they should have heeded the old Wall Street adage, *"Don't confuse brains with a bull market."*

Stock Market Prognosticators

Thousands of people make their livings by generating commissions or selling advisory newsletters that promote the concept of picking the right stocks and beating the market. The following four rules clear up some misconceptions about making market predictions.

Forecasting Rules:

1. It is very difficult to forecast, especially about the future.

2. He who lives by the crystal ball soon learns to eat ground glass.

3. The moment you forecast, you know you're going to be wrong – you just don't know when and in what direction.

4. If you're ever right, never let them forget it.

The "best" way to invest is still to take the conservative, long-term route with your important money. If you have extra money that you don't mind losing, go ahead and play the market. But, only play/speculate/gamble with that relatively small sum and no more. Then, if you are successful within the bull market you can say, "me too" when talking to other market "players." But, by being wise with how you've handled your important money, you can avoid that forlorn "me too" when everyone else is complaining about heavy losses.

Slow and Steady

The road to success in the market is to buy quality investments in a diversified portfolio, and rebalance when appropriate. James Whiddon gives this advice: "Once we have a portfolio set up properly, we rebalance it every six months. One asset class may have done better than another on the equity side. When we rebalance, we 'chop off' the part that has grown and redistribute among the equities that haven't grown so fast or perhaps lost value. Consequently, we are always selling high(er) and buying low(er) with this action."

James Harris III has a similar philosophy, "I think the best way to make money is not to lose money; the best way not to lose money is have three to five different asset categories and, at the same time, to rebalance on a regular basis."

Greed

"Bulls make money. Bears make money. Pigs get slaughtered."

"Losing potential profits hurts only the ego; losing money really hurts."

"Don't let the tail wag the dog."

Barbara Hudock tells the story of a retired client who refused to follow her advice because he didn't want to pay taxes on his investments. "He had approximately $200 thousand in CDs, bonds, and annuities. He told me he needed more income. He had accumulated a large amount of stock from the utility company through the employee stock purchase plan and, because of takeovers and mergers, the stock was now up to over $2 million in value but paid little, if any, income. We told him he needed to diversify. We created a balanced portfolio for him, but he decided against it. His reason? He was going to have to pay taxes on it. I said, 'Yes, you're going to have to pay long-term, capital-gain taxes. We can't get around that.'

"I explained the fees that go with a managed account program and provided documentation on three separate occasions of what we recommended he do. He never did it. Now, with the drop in the technology market, the stock is worthless. He went from being worth $2.5 million in assets to less than $300,000 almost overnight because he didn't want to pay taxes and commissions on the stock. We encourage people, but we can't force people. Of course we're not perfect, but it's our job to help clients to the best of our abilities and, in this case, the lack of diversification devastated his portfolio."

Ouch!

"The stock market is that creation of man that humbles him the most."

Many investors who have lost money in the market now realize their strategic or tactical errors and are searching for an investment professional who can show them the way to achieve their goals.

The aftermath of poor investment decision-making is emotional scarring and the desire to assign blame. Sometimes investors feel personal shame for their decisions or are embarrassed that they trusted someone who, in hindsight, was simply a great salesperson. A good advisor won't criticize you, but will help you identify and learn from your mistakes. They will help you outline your goals, craft an Investment Policy Statement and find the right approaches so mistakes don't happen again.

But, If You Won't Listen to Logic

What happens when you get caught up in the crowd and change your investment objectives and parameters? If your advisor cannot reach you with logic, define reasonable expectations, or convince you of the need for appropriate asset allocation, it may be time to part ways.

In Conclusion

"No profession requires more hard work, intelligence, patience, and mental discipline than successful investing."

CONNELL ON INTEGRITY

"**A**t the core of our investment philosophy is the belief that dedication to a strict investment discipline must be combined with an unwavering commitment to superior client service."

George Connell Jr., CIMA
Washington Investment Advisors

CHAPTER 16

Monitoring & Benchmarking
Portfolio Performance

M onitoring portfolio performance is discussed from two perspectives: 1) A brief overview of how advisors review the portfolio performance of money managers they work with, and 2) Comments and discussions from advisors on key factors that you should be aware of when monitoring investment performance.

Monitoring a portfolio or monitoring portfolio managers is a process that is too complicated to explore in depth in this book. However, you should know that special, highly sophisticated computer programs are used to "crunch the numbers" to discover the true risk-reward relationships within a particular portfolio. By using this technology along with their sophisticated professional training and extensive experience, advisors are able to correctly interpret and analyze investment data.

Ask your advisor about any or all of the following monitoring tools and programs:

- Asset Allocation
- Multi-Disciplinary Portfolios
- Style Analysis
- Attribution Analysis

- Sector Allocation

- Market Analysis

- PIPODs (Popular Index Portfolio Distribution[1])

- Client Risk Analysis

It's important to keep in mind that every financial vehicle – stocks, bonds, insurance, business valuations, real estate, gold, paintings, etc. – is cyclical. The cycles often depend on the state of the economy, inflation/deflation rates, political policies, military actions, societal influences, global events, as well as overall investor psychology. Be aware that when some investment vehicles are going down, others are going up. Asset allocation tries to optimally balance or blend the investment vehicles so that your long-term objectives are achieved without undue risk on your portfolio.

Over-weighting your portfolio with a particular stock or industry group poses an often-hidden risk. Imagine that your portfolio should have no more than 2 percent of its money in large capitalization stocks. You might purchase different types of mutual funds to balance your portfolio only to find that many of the funds actually include some of the same top 100 or 500 stocks. Since individual stocks can have different attributes, one mutual fund manager may view IBM, for example, as a large capitalization stock, another could see it as a long-term growth stock, while another might views it as a core stock. All three funds may hold the stock for different purposes. You, however, may happen to own all three funds and find yourself with two to 10 times more IBM than would be appropriate. Asset allocation software can discover these over-weighting problems.

Reginald Armstrong speaks to the same problem when he says, "The vast amount of portfolios I review have overlapping investments. Some, for example, have four money managers that are all fishing out of the same pond — no diversification." He says it's important to ask if your portfolio is helping you accomplish your goals. "By and large, most investors don't know — they have a portfolio, they are trying to make money, and they have goals that they haven't really crystallized." He continues, "Investors need to crystallize their goals in 3-D [Dreams, Dollars, Deadlines], then get a good idea of whether or not their portfolio has the potential to do what you want it to." He and his company provide a before-and-after picture that shows what can occur. They find that only 10 to15 percent of investor portfolios are on track, while 85 percent are not. And of those that are on track, the majority have inefficient portfolios. As Armstrong says, "Investors could be doing things a lot smarter."

The ideal blend of return versus risk is often shown in an "Efficient Frontier" diagram. This diagram, provided by Donald DeWees Jr., shows that the asset mix in the lower left corner takes on less risk and expects less return than the asset mix in the upper right corner, which takes on higher risk and expects a higher return. According to DeWees, "The asset mix best suited for you will depend on your unique investment goals and tolerance for risk. In 1954, our founder, James Wheat, said (in part), 'depression and adversity strike without warning from a clear sky. There are no signals.' His pro-phetic statement reinforces one of our core beliefs that we should not expose clients to more risk than may be necessary to achieve their fi-nancial goals."

A Model Portfolio

Both Armstrong and DeWees speak to the unique portfolio needs of each individual investor. Yet, most large financial firms offer "model portfolios" that are suppose to con-tain the ideal mix of stocks, bonds, and cash for different investment goals. As Brent Bentrim comments, "It's easier [for the large financial firms] to mass market near-fits." He goes on to describe how "the aver-age wire house has only five model portfolios for all clients. "In real-ity, we need to have technology to better assist advisors to determine whether or not the money managers they use are value-added to the client in regard to the client's unique goal, not the firm's model portfo-lio," he says.

Using a mass-market model portfolio can be like getting a suit off the rack without any additional tailoring. The real question is not whether a model portfolio is good or bad, but how it benefits you if all of your other assets (real estate, insurances, etc.) aren't considered in the equa-tion. Stated another way, how can a tailor fit a suit to you if half the fabric is missing? A portfolio that takes into account your total financial situation is more likely to achieve specific goals.

Bentrim explains his process of creating a customized portfolio and setting appropriate benchmarks to monitor performance. "Once we know a client's goals with the sophisticated financial planning software, we have an idea of what a client's minimal acceptance rate of return is to meet their goals. Based on the client's resources, assets, and everything they've got, we can then figure out that a 5.5 percent minimum return, for instance, is needed each year to achieve their goals. That scenario includes inflation fees, taxes, etc.

"We then create a unique benchmark for the client. For example: how, over the last 76 years of watching the market, would a portfolio need to be allocated to return 5.3 percent each year? We then answer that question. We look back at real numbers, instead of pontificating that what happened in the past will repeat; we focus in on what could happen. We let clients know they will need to put X amount of large cap value, Y amount of large cap growth, Z amount of high-yield bonds, etc. to be able to make 5.5 percent with a 99 percent probability of reaching their goal.

"My firm uses a very sophisticated analytical tool. I can put in a blended portfolio versus a client's goal and then look at it with a historical probability of beating the goal on a regular basis. I also want to know the amount of times the portfolio has under-performed the goal."

Benchmarking Portfolio Performance

As discussed earlier in the book, a money manager should be given three to five years to perform. However, if a particular manager is consistently under-performing his peer group, that is, competitors with the same investment style and objectives (apples-to-apples measurement), your advisor will see a warning flag. Since your financial advisor is constantly monitoring all of the money managers he/she works with and is regularly scanning for other good managers, it becomes evident when performance is missing the mark. At that point, other measures will be used to determine if the problem is major or minor. No matter what, that manager will be watched more closely.

Consistent performance is an important consideration. The manager should consistently outperform a benchmark or a peer group. If not, an advisor needs to ask "Why not?" and look for an answer. An advisor checks different standard performance ratios to determine specifically how or where the underperformance is occurring. They'll also look at factors such as change of personnel, structure of portfolio, differences in how they invest (known as style differences), and more to determine if the money manager firm is still appropriate for your investment objectives.

There are many ways to evaluate a manager. Probably the most popular method is in "relative terms," meaning if a particular manager, for example, has been hired to manage money allocated to small-capitalization, defensive stocks, then he/she should be doing better than most of his/her competitors who manage the same type of stock portfolio.

The most appropriate course of action is usually to keep a money manager unless there are compelling reasons to change. If another manager can do a better job for you, however, the advisor would recommend a change.

Popular Versus Customized Benchmarks

Most investors are only familiar with a small portion of the benchmarks used in the financial services industry. The most popular benchmarks or indexes are: Dow Jones Industrial Average, Standard & Poor's 500, and the Russell Index.

What is the Greatest Risk?

DeWees Investment Consulting Group of Wachovia Securities' informational white paper explains that not attaining your objectives may be the greatest risk of all. It says:

"We believe the greatest risk for most investors is not meeting their objectives! Many financial advisors try to identify their client's maximum risk tolerance, then design portfolios to avoid that level of risk. However, we believe investors prefer to avoid risk, but begrudgingly accept it based on the life-style tradeoffs required to avoid it (save more, spend less). This makes the definition of a client's risk tolerance a trade-off decision totally separate from a theoretical or projected return. When facing the decision about how much risk to take, one can only rationally base this decision on what it means to them personally. By checking a box that says 20 percent downside risk, particularly for wealthy investors, most advisors would position their client's portfolio with far more risk than is needed to have a high probability of meeting their goals.

In contrast, investors whose wealth and life-style goals strain their portfolio's likelihood to succeed, end up in portfolios that are too conservative, forcing them to save more money, and possibly altering their life style, than would be needed if they assumed investment risk beyond their stated risk tolerance. We believe investors in this position would be willing to accept more investment risk (than initially assumed) by looking at it as a return trade-off, if in doing so, they were aware of the impact it might have on their life style (spend more, or save less). This is an entirely different view of risk versus return for most investors and their advisors."

Each of these averages has strengths and weaknesses. They don't all measure the same thing. Theoretically, you could have one going up and another going down on the same day! These are the indexes most often referred to in the media and, although popular, probably have no real value for individual investors. As a result, many advisors actually prepare customized benchmarks and/or indexes for their clients. The "Jack and Jill Jones index is up 3 percent this quarter versus inflation" is more meaningful if that index is based upon all of your holdings – stocks, bonds, CDs, real estate, cash value of insurance, business valuation, accounts receivable, etc.

A logical consequence of the "individualized index" described above, is the realization that each aspect of our portfolio must be separately measured against different benchmarks. Your small-capitalization manager must be measured against other small-capitalization managers, not value managers or large-cap managers, or the S&P 500 or anything else.

Key Factors to be Aware of

Heard on the news: *"The market is up 15 percent from its lows, increasing the probability that we will see a sustained rally."* This sounds like great news, but is little comfort if you bought when the market was substantially higher.

Chapter 14 discusses the fact that if you were able to look back on the graph of the market over a long time frame you would always be looking downward. Why, then, would you even be concerned about the mathematics of profits and losses? It's because you need to look at various benchmarks relative to *your* starting time and money. The second reason is you need to remember the importance of a diversified portfolio so that you immunize yourself to the risks described below.

People can lose sight of risk when monitoring or managing their portfolios. They fail to appreciate that when a portfolio declines by 50 percent, it takes a 100 percent increase in value to get back to even. Eight out of 10 people on the street don't understand that when you lose 50 percent, you need more than a 50 percent gain to get back up there [to your starting point].

Jacques Abrams explains what severe declines in the market really mean to an investor. He sites recent history. "The NASDAQ, which until recently, was down somewhere on the order of 70 percent from its March 2000 high, has resulted in these investments diminishing in value from 100 cents on the dollar to 30 cents on the dollar. Now it takes an increase of 333 percent to get back to where they were. Another example is the S&P 500, which has been down about 50 percent the last three years and up 20 percent this year. The newspapers and talk-show hosts tout the 20 percent upswing. However, when you really look more closely at the numbers, it's not 20 percent from the original starting point but only 10 percent. There's 'sizzle' in the 20 percent figure, but the reality is that the market still has fallen 40 percent from where it was three years ago.[2]"

Your Comfort Zone

After you have had the opportunity to work with an advisor, learn about his/her process and had a portfolio customized to your particular needs, two important things remain:

1. Let the advisor do his job

2. Don't micro-manage

David Bromelkamp offers this analogy: Investing is like planting a tree. Clients left to their own devices will try to make the tree grow faster. But when you plant a tree, you should only water it once a day. Over watering can kill a tree. Investing is something that you cannot try hard at it. It is a passive activity. You buy and wait for five years and sell it.

In Conclusion

Investing is like planting a tree...

All of the methodical monitoring and benchmarking processes described in this chapter gives your advisor the tools to ensure that your goals will be achieved. Don't rush things, or resist your advisor's well-thought-out plan. Just sit back, relax, and enjoy the process. Soon your tree will be giving you great shade and comfort.

---

1. PIPODs was developed by Ron Surz of PPCA and is a useful tool in manager evaluation and unique within the industry.
2. Here is the mathematics behind the illustration. A hypothetical index starts at 1,000 and falls by 50% to 500. It then appreciates 20% to 600. But, it is still down 40% from the original 1,000.

Parker on Integrity

"In light of recent financial scandals and corporate malfeasance, the *integrity* question, as it should be, is front and center in the minds of consumers of financial services. Every time I sit down with someone searching for a (new) financial advisor, I can feel the fire of those sinners that have walked before me. It's an interrogative atmosphere in which I almost expect the prospective client to offer me a cigarette as I'm blinded by the light that is actually their assumed mistrust (obviously a learned behavior).

Fortunately, I refuse the 'smoke' and am able to dim the lights with a simple question: 'Do you know that I have been awarded the Chartered Financial Analyst™ or CFA® designation, a financial designation founded upon the Code of Ethics and a Standard of Professional Conduct that ensures that the client's interest is the only interest that matters?' A fellow CFA® charter holder was appointed chairman of the SEC to rid the financial community of the ills that cause the same mistrust that I can read in your eyes right now."

Donald R. Parker, CFA®, AVA
Gryphon Valuation Consultants

CHAPTER 17

The Importance of Advisor Education

"Who Knows What?" and "Why Is It Important to You?"

An advisor's experiences, designations and the extent of continuing education are useful ways to judge his/her potential value as an advisor. It is also important to realize, however, that *a designation or degree does not automatically equal competence and caring.* You can only determine those traits through your due diligence. That said, any advisor—from a large or small firm—who goes beyond the norm to earn professional designations, regularly attends continuing education seminars to maintain their designations, and subscribes to a stringent code of ethics, should stand far above others.

For discerning investors searching for a high-level advisor, the only competition for one high-level advisor is *another* high-level advisor There are tens of thousands less knowledgeable, non-credentialed, and less experienced advisors who may also be able to assist you in some form, but can you afford to take the chance?

These three simple analogies make this point. Would you take your brand new car to an auto mechanic who doesn't like to deal with those new-fangled, computer-chip thing-a-ma-bobbers? Would you want to retain an attorney who hasn't kept up with case law or go to a doctor who hasn't kept up with medical advances? Chances are, you wouldn't choose to go to any of them unless your needs were truly simple or you didn't care what kind of service you received.

It is hard to imagine any affluent investor using the services of anyone other than a high-level financial advisor. Donald R. Parker makes a salient comment: "The fact is, anyone can hang out their shingle and call himself or herself an investment advisor. That's why it is so important for investors to be familiar with the various designations and what they mean."

Deciphering Alphabet Soup

The list of financial services industry associations and organizations providing designations is so long that there is not room to list them all here. Each has different, yet overlapping, services. Depending on your financial needs, different designations, degrees or organizations, would be more applicable than others. For example, if you are looking for portfolio management and evaluation services, consider a Certified Investment Management Analyst (CIMA), Certified Investment Management Consultant (CIMC) or Chartered Financial Analysts™ (CFA®). For financial planning services, CFA®, CPA, Chartered Financial Consultant (ChFC), and Chartered Life Underwriter (CLU) designations may be more important to consider. Parker, a CFA®, told us that "the legendary investor Benjamin Graham helped establish the CFA® program in the early 60s, and today it is the only globally recognized mark of achievement for the highest level of ethics, education, and experience amongst financial professionals."

To learn more about each designation, including its educational requirements, code of standards/ethics, practitioners in your area, call the organization(s) or visit their Web sites. (Brief description of common industry designations are provided at the end of this chapter.)

Financial Services Industry - Designations	
CFA® www.aimr.org	Chartered Financial Analyst 800-247-8132
CFP® www.cfp.net	Certified Financial Planner™ 888-237-6275
ChFC www.amercol.edu	Chartered Financial Consultant 888-263-7265

CIMA www.imca.org	Certified Investment Mgmt Analyst 303-770-3377
CIMC www.imca.org	Certified Investment Mgmt Consultant [1] 303-770-3377
CIS www.imca.org	Certified Investment Strategist 303-770-3377
CLU www.amercol.edu	Chartered Life Underwriter 888-263-7265
CPA www.aicpa.org	Certified Public Accountant 888-777-7077
CPTx www.fraudpro.com	Certified Practitioner of Taxation 408-274-7390
CSA www.society-csa.com	Certified Senior Advisor 888-653-1785
IFA www.cfstudies.com	Investment Fiduciary Auditor 412-390-5080
PFS www.aicpa.org	Personal Financial Specialist 888-777-7077
RIA www.sec.gov/iard	Registered Investment Advisor 202-942-0691

ChFC and CLU designee Frederick Dawson gives this advice regarding designations: "One of the first things I recommend to investors is that they seek out a person who is qualified by education and, at a minimum, holds a Certified Financial Planner™ (CFP®) designation. I prefer someone who has a ChFC and CLU. We all suffer from alphabet soup around here. A couple of my partners are CFPs®, one is a CFP®, CLU, ChFC, and MBA. He suffers from excessive education (he laughs). I definitely recommend that people search out someone who holds designations not only for the fact they know they are striving to be educated, but they are also held to a high degree of ethics. They are committed to learning what they should be doing for their clients."

It's not necessarily important that an advisor hold a particular designation. The important thing is that he/she has access to an internal or external team of professionals who have the knowledge and skills needed to help you achieve your objectives.

In addition to learning what the designations mean, James Harris III suggests that you ask the advisor to explain the course of study required for the designation or degree, their continuing education requirements or personal program for on-going education, what strengths and weaknesses the designation implies, and then how it all applies to your particular situation.

Checking an Advisor's Disciplinary History

George Connell Jr. suggests that before you interview an advisor, you should get answers to questions such as: Are there any legal filings against the advisor? Has the advisor been sued or has there been mismanagement within the firm?

The following Web sites and telephone numbers can help you in this search.

Certified Financial Planner Board of Standards, Inc.
888-237-6275   www.CFP.net
North American Securities Administration
202-737-900   www.nasaa.org
National Association of Insurance Commissioners
816-842-3600   www.naic.org
National Association of Securities Dealers Regulation
800-289-9999   www.nasdr.com
National Fraud Exchange (fee involved)
800-289-0416
Securities and Exchange Commission
202-942-7040   www.sec.gov

Checking on an advisor's credentials and looking up any disciplinary history are important steps in the process. However, you may wish to go a step further. Connell suggests [although his list has been expanded somewhat] that you also consider checking whether the advisor has received recognition in his/her field, such as:

- Did the advisor receive any industry or community awards? Barbara Hudock, for example, was awarded the Dalbar Financial Professional Seal; Parker was named by Nelson's as one of the "World's Top 20 Best Portfolio Managers" in 2000.

- Has he/she spoken at a conference of peers? Jeffrey Thomas teaches classes on fiduciary responsibilities at a university; David Bromeklamp is a frequent speaker at conferences for nonprofit institutions, attorney's CPAs, etc. John Chiacchiero is an adjunct lecturer at the University of South Carolina-Beaufort.

- Has the advisor published articles or books? Dawson has been published nationally and internationally more than 350 times.

- Has the advisor been referenced in articles or books?

- Has the advisor receive industry or community recognition?

- Is the advisor held in high esteem by other professionals and peers?

Community involvement is another way advisors can distinguish themselves. Some of the organizations that benefit from the involvement of our advisors – or any interested person — include: Rotary, Kiwanis, Boy Scouts and Girl Scouts of America, Big Brothers-Big Sisters, health-related charitable organizations, community-oriented causes, youth sports groups, and the list goes on. These organizations make a positive difference in the lives of many.

The Value of Continuing Education

In this rapidly changing investment world, new products, services, and investment strategies are constantly being developed. While high-level advisors who hold industry designations have had stringent continuing education requirements for many years, regulatory authorities only recently have imposed minimal (and, rather nebulous) continuing education requirements on the balance of the financial services industry.

Ira Rapaport's comment sums it up: "Designations [and degrees] are important. Investors should want to work with an advisor who has taken the time to make a commitment to the profession. They want to work with someone who is competent and who has been properly trained, licensed, and regularly participates in continuing education programs. Someone who puts in the time on an annual basis to stay current and fresh is a head above those who don't."

The following brief descriptions of industry designations was obtained from www.mutualfunds.about/com

Accredited Asset Management Specialist (AAMS) This designation is awarded by the College for Financial Planning and persons obtaining this title must complete a self study course and pass an examination on asset management topics.

Certified Financial Planner™ (CFP®) The CFP designation is not easy to obtain. Professionals with a CFP designation will have broad knowledge of all aspects of financial planning. The CFP must undergo years of testing and continuing education.

Certified Fund Specialist (CFS) This designation is offered by the Institute of Business and Finance (IBF) to financial services professionals who successfully complete its course and pass the comprehensive exam. This designation focuses on mutual funds.

Certified Investment Management Analyst (CIMA) This certification requires coursework and a final exam and is administered by the Investment Management Consultants Association plus 3 years experience in the investment consulting field.

Certified Investment Specialist (CIS) CIMAs that go one step further obtain the CIS designation. It requires advanced concepts and strategies in asset analysis, tax planning and legal issues pertaining to investment consultants.

Certified Public Accountant (CPA) Becoming a CPA is no easy task. Besides obtaining an accounting degree, CPAs must meet a 150-hour requirement and pass a four part exam. CPAs can offer financial services, but their specialty is tax issues.

Personal Financial Specialist (PFS) CPAs that want to focus more on financial planning obtain a PFS designation. They must have at least 250 hours of yearly experience in financial planning and have passed an additional exam.

Chartered Financial Analyst™ (CFA®) This designation is one of the toughest to obtain. The CFA has passed three examinations and accumulated three years of professional work experience. This is a common designation for mutual fund managers, money managers and stock analysts.

Chartered Investment Counselor (CIC) Professionals with a CIC designation must obtain a CFA designation first, be employed by a member of the ICAA (Investment Counsel Association of America), and must have 5 cumulative years of related work experience.

Chartered Financial Consultant (ChFC) Similar to CFPs, the Chartered Financial Consultant must complete multiple years worth of examinations and has knowledge in all areas including tax, estate, insurance, financial planning and portfolio management. ChFCs tend to come from the insurance industry.

Chartered Life Underwriter (CLU) Professionals with a CLU designation have completed a ten course curriculum covering life insurance products.

Chartered Mutual Fund Counselor (CMFC) To obtain this designation you must complete a self-study program and final examination on different mutual fund topics. Professionals with this designation provide mutual fund advice to clients.

Chartered Retirement Planning Counselor (CRPC) This designation is usually obtained by financial advisors that want to increase their knowledge of pre and post retirement financial planning.

Chartered Retirement Plans Specialist (CRPS) This designation is usually obtained by financial advisors that want to increase their technical skills in administering retirement plans for business clients.

Registered Investment Advisor (RIA) These professionals generally charge a flat fee and/or an ongoing asset-based fee for their investment management services and are registered with the SEC. The SEC does not formally recognize "RIA" as an official title because they don't want to imply that advisors had to be certified.

Many of the advisors commented that they love the intellectual challenge of ongoing education and regularly made statements similar to "you just can't know enough." Here are some examples from advisors interviewed for this book:

- All are members of various industry associations.

- Some attend meetings/conferences from other disciplines to explore new concepts. For example, Abrams attends estate planning classes for attorneys. He realizes that it gives him valuable information and an edge.

- A few are officers of associations. For example, Dawson is the past president of the Delaware chapter of the Society of Financial Service Professionals; Parker formed a CFA group in Nevada; Bromelkamp is on the Board of Directors of the Minnesota Society of CPAs and is president of the Twin Cities Chapter of Investment Management Cconsultant Association (IMCA).

- All involve staff members in ongoing professional education, whether it's required or not.

Many times an advisor's commitment to education requires a rather large financial expenditure. "I spend literally thousands of dollars and a couple hundred hours every year on my continuing education," says Matthew Potter. "With the different licenses and designations I have, I know the value of constantly upgrading my knowledge. It allows me to provide more sophisticated information to my clients.

Experience Counts … *a lot!*

In the previous chapter we commented that wisdom comes from experience, and experience comes from mistakes. The question is, where do you want your advisor to be on the learning/experience curve? In other words, on an experience scale from 0 to 10, where do you want your advisor and advisory team to be?

0	1	2	3	4	5	6	7	8	9	10

"0" indicates no experience; "5" means fairly experienced/knowledgeable; "10" means very experienced/knowledgeable.

If you're like most investors, you want a highly experienced advisor and advisory team handling your money. After all, why should an advisor gain "experience" at your expense? This need/demand for experience doesn't have to preclude you from working with most new advisors. If the new advisor has a mentor or someone sitting in on and checking his/her work, you probably don't have much cause for concern. If you do choose a new advisor, just make sure that the experience of the firm is behind him/her. Sometimes the new, younger advisors have had more up-to-date training in the financial services arena and can provide some innovative approaches to dealing with your financial matters.

In Conclusion

Experience and education should be highly rated factors in selecting your advisor. High-level advisors who have sought and maintain industry designations demonstrate a commitment to professionalism.

---

1. The CIMC designation was offered by the Institute of Certified Investment Management Consultants (ICIMC) , which merged with the Investment Management Consultants Association (IMCA)

2. The Dalbar Financial Professional Seal is awarded to financial professionals who have met the standards in client performance, trust and satisfaction, and have the prerequisite experience, regulatory record and size of practice.

CHIACCHIERO ON INTEGRITY

"*Integrity* means doing the right thing when no one is watching. This is a personal relationship business based upon trust and confidence. This means you must always do what is right for your client even if it is easier not to."

John Chiacchiero
The Wealth Management Group
Melhado, Flynn & Associates, Inc.

The Educated Investor

A television commercial for Men's Warehouse (clothing store) carries the tagline, "An educated consumer is our best customer." A high-level advisor has two similar desires: "An educated investor is the best client," and "An educated client is the best investor."

Jeffrey Thomas probably sums it up best for all of the other advisors when he says, "I am always more happy working with an educated investor because I can talk to them at a level they really will understand. 'You should consider harvesting some gains over here, and put it in another asset class.' An informed investor understands the validity of those rebalancing techniques."

Advisors repeatedly emphasize the need for client education, the pleasure they receive from teaching people, and the mutual benefits derived from such education. All the advisors interviewed for this book make a concerted effort to enhance their clients' level of knowledge using a variety of methods: educational seminars, newsletters, personal meetings, meetings with a client's professional advisors, and investment seminars where clients meet money managers.

These advisors make the same commitment to educating clients as they do to gain ongoing professional development for themselves and staff members. In many cases, client education goes beyond learning about the financial plan or how money managers work; it sometimes expands to a more comprehensive education.

Client Education: It's Essential

All of the advisors interviewed for this book feel that client education is critical in a financial planning relationship. They all have numerous examples of how they keep in touch with their clients and teach them as much as they can about the financial process. Because of space limitations, we could only include a few here.

Frederick Dawson goes the extra mile to educate some of his clients with special needs. The following story also serves as a wake-up call for all family members to pursue a basic financial education.

He says, "When I look around, I see a lot of divorced and widowed women whose husbands said, 'I'll take care of you for the rest of your life. You have nothing to worry about.' The husbands wrote the checks, paid the bills, and everything else that was necessary and left them in the dark. And, unfortunately, these women accepted it. As a consequence, I sometimes have women coming to me who don't know how to balance a checkbook, don't understand what a financial statement is or how to ana-

Barbara B. Hudock, managing principal, Hudock Moyer Financial Advisors, presents an innovative approach to client education. We created a JULIET Society —Just Us Ladies Intelligently Eating Together. It came out of a group of retired physician clients who created the ROMEO Club (Retired Old Men Eating Out). Every Thursday they have lunch together and the group has grown nicely. Some of the women in the community were talking about the guys being at the Romeo Club, so we decided to create a Juliet Society. It is open to all women in the area. At the meetings, we have lunch and discuss financial topics. One week we may talk about 529 plans, the next about the Envision Process, a retirement-goal-planning process. Most of the time I lead it. Sometimes we'll have a member of my team participate as a guest speaker. It's a nice little social hour for them, but they enjoy learning as well.

Hudock's educational commitment to her clients is not limited to the weekly Juliet Society luncheons. "We hold educational events for our clients. We want them to walk out feeling like they've been well informed. When people participate as a group, it creates a different, very productive atmosphere and a willingness to ask questions. It helps them to understand various financial topics, so that when they make a decision they can say, "Yes I understand that now."

lyze it. We work to build their confidence. We help them understand the intricacies of their financial matters. Now they walk in and show me all these things they are doing. They write the checks, balance their checkbooks, and they're taking control of their lives. One proudly said, 'I went out and bought my first new car.' I just beam with joy to see them taking control of their lives."

Varioius Approaches to the Educational Process

Financial advisors find their jobs rewarding because of the difference they can make in peoples' lives. Dawson sums it up saying, "I love this business! I love helping people. I get such a charge out of seeing the lights come on in their eyes when they realize, "Oh, that's how that works."

Barbara Hudock and her team regularly send out questionnaires that poll their clients on a variety of topics, including whether they would like to attend a series of educational events. "Clients value education. They may not retain it all, but it makes them feel they are part of the process." Hudock explains that sometimes the topics they offer at the educational seminars may not be applicable to a client, but they will often walk away saying they want their children or grandchildren to know about the topics we've discussed. "It gives clients a sense of control and involvement in the investment process that is healthy for both them and us," she says.

Jacques Abrams approaches education through individual client meetings and semi-annual seminars. "I bring my clients through a quasi-formal educational process. I try to provide them with some historical perspective regarding stock market returns, volatility, performance of portfolio managers and expenses. This historical information is complemented with more immediate information regarding investments, economic information, and reminders about factors such as reversion to the mean and diversification." He continues, "I also try to provide them with some perspective on investment philosophies and the integration of various elements of investments as they relate to estate planning, taxes, insurance, long-term care, emotional well-being, etc. In a comprehensive financial planning sense, the document I produce for people at the beginning of an engagement provides an initial template for the long-term. I'm not sure clients understand all the intricacies of the planning process, especially estate planning, no matter how many times we go through it. Nevertheless, there is something to be said for repetition, learning, and the challenge to effectively communicate in a manner that each client can understand." From a slightly different perspective, in the final analysis, Abrams says, "While I might serve as a personal CFO for clients, they inevitably 'live' with the results that our relationship has cultivated. I believe I have the responsibility to educate so that, within reason, they can make the best-informed decision."

Donald DeWees Jr. comments, "I hold a series of regular and ongoing seminars quarterly called "Meet Your Manager." At our last event, 75 high-end retail and small institutional clients attended. I do a capital market review, try to put things in a historical perspective, I give them my outlook and introduce the manager. The manager talks about his philosophy and discipline in managing their respective strategy in a multi-manager portfolio. We then open it up for a Q&A. We try to do these seminars three or four times per year."

James Harris III something similar. He invites clients to dinner with the institutional or separate account managers. It gives his clients a chance to meet with core portfolio managers, international managers, and to learn how they make decisions. Investors also get a chance to ask questions.

As Harris adds, "We explain everything to our clients – asset allocation, diversification, choosing and monitoring performance of managers, etc. They have to know that I don't have discretion on the account, so I have to explain everything to them so they have a full understanding of my thought processes and the step-by-step decisions that I make. The only way to do this is to fully educate them."

You can take an active role in seeking education from your advisor by doing the following:

- Letting the advisor know about your needs and expectations.

- Asking the advisor to explain any part of the process you don't understand.

- Making sure the advisor communicates on a level that you easily understand.

- Asking the advisor about seminars and other ways to learn more about managing your money.

When searching for an advisor, you should ask the candidate to describe his/her last educational event and what topics and material were covered. Also, ask for references of people who have participated in the advisor's educational process.

Many advisors send out regular mailings to their clients. These range from the monthly *Curran Views* newsletter that was referenced in Chapter 14 to more informal e-mail updates. These advisors consider ongoing client education a critical part of their jobs.

Special Education Needs

Douglas Aldridge and Jack Krapf work with many foundations and pension plans, which means they are in contact with many people who have fiduciary responsibilities. Most people are not well-versed in high finance and in the intricacies of various financial instruments. This, they note, is also true of many trustees who sit on investment committees, foundations, and pension plans. Aldridge and Krapf realize that part of their role in these situations is to provide ongoing education on topics such as:

- Identifying specific, measurable financial objectives
- Portfolio management techniques
- Writing Investment Policy Statements
- Asset allocation, asset classes, asset management
- Roles and services of investment managers
- How to analyze managers and appropriately review quantitative analysis

Essentially, they help teach trustees how to make informed decisions and make education a high priority and an ongoing process.

Aldridge and Krapf further explain, "I think it's very important that an institutional-type client, run by a board and having fiduciary responsibility, must be guided by competent people who have an understanding of investments. And, if they don't understand how portfolios are run, at least they are open-minded and will listen to the experts and not be swayed by peer pressure. I find it amazing how many people are serving on boards and are in way over their heads. Here is a pool of assets being managed by a board being helped by a consultant, but the board members don't listen because they don't understand the ramifications of the decisions they make. Whoever is responsible for putting these boards together should, from a fiduciary standpoint and for the benefit of those involved, get people who are competent. They shouldn't be political appointments. They need good people who understand investing."

In Conclusion

Krapf comments that the worst situation is when someone comes to him, gives him money and says, "Just make me money." He explains, "We don't want those types of clients any more. We don't want clients who refuse to talk about risk return. In situations such as these, there is no meeting of the minds."

As an investor, you owe it to yourself to continually increase your level of financial understanding. You don't have to be an expert, but you need to know what's going on with your finances. Make sure that any advisor you deal with actively tries to help you increase your level of financial sophistication. An advisor should never use the "black box" approach, meaning they don't reveal any of their investment strategies and tools to you.

As an investor, you have a moral obligation to *learn*. If you are a trustee of any sort, then you also need to research and abide by your fiduciary responsibilities.

Throughout this book, we have introduced ideas, topics, techniques, and approaches used by high-level advisors. It is now your responsibility to take action so that you learn more about these investment ideas and tools from your advisor.

POTTER ON INTEGRITY

"I once heard someone say that *integrity* is doing the right thing when no one is watching. When a financial advisor is entrusted with the duty of helping clients manage their money, *integrity* is not just a nice quality, it is an essential part of the everyday workings of the advisor. The client must be able to trust that her advisor is going to do what is best for her every time, all the time. It is too easy for someone in a position of influence, like a financial advisor, to do things that may be good for the advisor, but questionable for the client. The integrity of the advisor must be unquestionable, so that even when the client is not looking over the advisor's shoulder, the right thing will be done."

Matthew N. Potter, CFP®, CIMC
Raymond James Financial Services

Wisdom from Experience

Scattered throughout this book are examples of typi-cal (and atypical) mistakes that investors make with investments. The word "mistake" has a harsh connotation to it – almost as if it *should have* been avoided and is some-thing to be ashamed of. Instead, you should look at a mis-take as a learning opportunity that leads to wisdom.

It has been said that wisdom comes from experience, and experience comes come mistakes. Another saying suggests that there are three kinds of people in the world: the fool—who makes a mistake and then continues to make the same mistake over and over again; the average person—who makes a mistake, sees the mistake, and says, "I'm not going to make that mistake again," and the wise person—who has been watching the mistakes of the oth-ers and says, "I'm not going to make those mistakes." Regardless of the type of person you were, the question now becomes, what type of person do you want to be from this day forward?

The wisdom born of experience and learning opportu-nities is illustrated in the lessons that follow.

- The biggest trap for the individual investor is get-ting caught in the psychology of the crowd. This trap is difficult to avoid because investors are inundated with messages to get in or to get out of the market "while the getting is good." That is why statistics show mutual fund sales are strong in the last part of a bull market (near the market peak) and redemptions strong near the market trough of a bear market. The adage to remember is, "The more widely held the belief in the permanence of the existing trend, the less likely it is to continue."

• Many investors are driven by fear and/or greed. Fear can make an investor afraid to take losses or to pay taxes. Greed often results in waiting for a stock to go up a little higher before the investor will sell it. In either case, fear or greed can chew at your savings and cause your financial plan to crumble.

• Under-diversification is common in many financial portfolios. Many investors put most or all of their money into their company's common stock – whether they are owners or employees of that company. The rationale is that they see how the company is faring, and they know the company's business approach. The problem is not investing in the company, but investing *too much* in one company.

• You, the investor, should use logic to drive your financial decisions. Logic means using a long-term approach and diversifying your portfolio to attain your specific goals.

• Selection of an investment advisor should result from actively searching for qualified people and then choosing one based on specific criteria outlined in this book.

Additional Lessons

"Beware of costs, but realize that you get what you pay for."

Make sure you take into account more than up front costs when it comes to hiring an advisor or buying investment products. Thomas Curran says, "Too many investors, by not doing their due diligence, base their decision solely on cost." Other advisors gave similar advice and strongly caution all advisors to "compare apples to apples." Within many investments are hidden costs that are rarely accounted for. High-level advisors disclose all the fees associated with creating a financial plan and/or managing your investments. They make a strong effort to avoid any possible conflicts of interest such as getting supplementary income from certain investments or firms in the form of bonus trips to Europe, or award banquets, etc.

Going Forward with Realistic Expectations

Although realistic expectations were discussed in previous chapters, John Chiacchiero offers a different viewpoint. "I had a client who had about $1.2 million, lost most of it and came to me with a portfolio of $250,000, and all of it invested in 11 technology stocks. After our meeting, she was able to understand how important it was to start looking at her expenses and what was going to be realistic moving forward. Her first desire was to try and get back what she had. We had to subtly work around that over a couple of weeks until she finally accepted that it probably wasn't going to happen. The question then became, can we make what is left last the rest of her life and grow it a bit?"

Use Appropriate Benchmarks

George Connell Jr. looks at the total return of a portfolio and then determines if each component of the portfolio is contributing to the total return objective. He says, "For example, it would be a mistake taking one money manager's return (the one who was the high-risk advisor and was hugely successful this quarter) and benchmark his performance to the fixed-income manager whose job was not to have any variability or any change in the overall asset level. While it is fascinating to look at each money manager's rate of return, investors need to keep track of how each component performs within that manager's peer group."

Connell provides a list of the "Top Ten Mistakes Investors Make." He says he collected the list from peers and personal experience and it is not meant to represent every possible mistake one could make!

Top Ten Mistakes Investors Make

1. Taking too much risk with your investments.

2. Failing to consider the effects of inflation and taxes.

3. Underestimating life expectancy.

4. Failing to take advantage of the years immediately before retirement.

5. Focusing on your retirement account to the exclusion everything else.

6. Failing to consider long-term care needs.

7. Making large loans to family and friends.

8. Overestimating how much you can withdraw from your retirement account.

9. Over-managing a retirement account.

10. Underestimating expenses in retirement.

Timing the Market

It's natural to want "to buy low, sell high," but, is it rational to expect to do so? No, no, a thousand times no! Trying to time the market is speculating, not investing. Some people try to time their purchases of individual stocks; others try to time mutual funds investments. Frederick Dawson had a client who tried to bring market timing to a new level. "I have a client who wanted to 'market time' the money managers. He wanted the ability to shut it down on a whim and start it back up on a whim. Try as I may to make him understand this would be counterproductive, he just wasn't listening. He still would have me shut down his accounts and go to a cash position. Against my advice we did it, and then the market took off. He started them back up again, the market softened. It happened several times to the point he admitted to being his own worst enemy. He knew it, but there was nothing I could do to 'take the gun out of his hand.'"

Impatience

Dawson makes this observation about investor jitters: "The biggest problem investors have is being impatient. I've done a lot of handholding in the last few years, as I'm sure everyone in our business has. I spend a lot of time holding hands when clients are down 30 percent, and they hear someone on the radio say 'jump to X or X' I shudder to think about the next train wreck."

Micro-Managing

If you want to manage your own money, then do so. If you engage the services of a high-level advisor, then let him/her call the shots within the parameters you've jointly established. This doesn't mean you can't ask questions or check the progress of your account; just make sure you give your advisor the leeway he/she needs to manage your money.

Choosing the Wrong Advisor

If your brother is a stockbroker at a large wire house, you may feel obligated to let him manage your account. Of course, it may be the right decision if, after doing your due diligence, he/she is the best person for the job. But don't automatically assume that a relative or friend is a good advisor. You must decide if that person is the best one available to manage your investments. Is he/ she – or you – a highly trained, credentialed, experienced money manager? Does that expertise extend to all styles of investing?

Many family/friend advisors are well intentioned, but you must make sure that they are truly competent, and can create the best financial plan for you and direct your investments in the most efficient, cost-effective manner.

In Conclusion

Learn from the mistakes of others. To help prevent or minimize mistakes, part of your strategy should be to evaluate your advisor and your holdings with specific criteria so you know when you are shifting off course.

While the landscape of tomorrow's markets may not resemble today's, the fundamentals — quality, trust, accountability — remain timeless."

— Arthur Levitt, Former SEC Chairman
Columbia Law School speech, 1999

CHAPTER 20

Trust: The Bottom Line

What are the elements within "The Trust Equation"? This chapter summarizes some of the key elements in the equation and helps you draw your own conclusions regarding the level of professionalism you want and need when choosing and working with a financial advisor.

In addition to holding mandated federal and state licenses to sell certain financial products, some advisors decide to increase their level of knowledge by getting an advanced degree in finance and/or by becoming certified in one or more investment fields of study. Each designation requires different educational requirements and provides knowledge applicable to a specific aspect of the investment process. Continuing education -- whether mandatory to maintain a designation, or volunary for professional enrichment -- ensures that advisors are familiar with the latest industry advances.

Advisors combine their knowledge and experience with that of other professionals to create a comprehensive team (internal and/or external) that can meet your particular financial needs. High-level advisors deliver high levels of advice and professionalism by using specific manager selection and evaluation processes and by incorporating rebalancing and rechecking procedures. They include individual and group educational meetings that help you and other clients.

As an investor you were introduced to a PROCESS that helps you choose an advisor. Like the parts of the watch, these components are interdependent and work in conjunction with each other. The key points are reiterated here:

- **P**repare: This phase has two parts: 1) finding a competent and trustworthy advisor, and 2) identifying your goals, objectives, legacy and values. You can search for an advisor by contacting industry associations, asking other professionals for references, and evaluating the levels of service offered. Simultaneously, you should be identifying your long-term objectives by pinpointing the kind of lifestyle you want to enjoy, the legacy you want to leave, and what you want your money to do for you and your family. Identifying these objectives is probably the most important thing you can do because it sets the direction for everything else.

- **R**esearch/**R**eview: Initial and subsequent meetings with potential advisors will help you identify those who are in sync with your objectives. Ask the advisor's client references questions that relate to your situation. Verify that the advisor has regular meetings with them and provides educational support. Once you've spoken to a few people, you'll have a pretty good feel for the advisor.

- **O**bjectives: Even though identifying your financial objectives will probably occur during the first meeting, this is a separate process. The advisor will help clarify your goals, translate them to meaningful investment objectives, and begin the planning process to get you where you want to be. You want an advisor who asks a lot of in-depth questions and is genuinely concerned about you.

- **C**ommunicate: An ongoing process in which everyone communicates with each other. The advisor keeps you apprised of portfolio results and other changes that may affect you. In turn, you inform the advisor of any changes in your life.

- **E**xecute and **E**valuate: Once an investment plan has been formulated, implement it. Of course you may wish to get a second opinion. Evaluation of the initial plan (via second opinion) and ongoing evaluation will make sure that you remain on course. Look at measurable results versus benchmarks to help determine if the investment process is meeting your goals.

- **S**ystems: Sophisticated computer software allows the advisor to measure performance in many ways. However, system also includes personnel processes that provide you with education and periodic updates. Systems help ensure that nothing slips through the cracks.

- **S**ynchronization: Complex needs usually require a multi-disciplinary solution. Other professionals are used to supplement the services provided by the advisor. These other professionals can be ones you already work with and/or those recommended by the advisor.

As an investor, it is important to realize that investing is a logical, systematic, objective process, not one based on "irrational exuberance." Discipline and dedication are needed to accomplish your goals, and you must watch out for traps along the way. Gain investment wisdom by learning from the mistakes and experiences of others. In the meantime, upgrade your knowledge of the industry and investment processes from the educational opportunities your advisor offers.

You and your advisor must have contingency plans for everything: What if you or your spouse dies or becomes incapacitated? What if the advisor dies? Is there a competent professional to take his/her place, or will you have to begin the search process again? When you die, you want your life mission and legacy plans to be realized.

In conclusion

Your past, present and future choices determine your financial destiny. Choose wisely, and remember that not doing anything is probably the worst choice of all.

Jacques S. Abrams, CFP® CIMC
Abrams Financial Management

TEL: 781.237.7111

EMAIL: jabrams@abramsfin.com

LOCATION: Wellesley, MA

BIO: President and founder of Abrams Financial Management, Jacques "Jack" S. Abrams has 28 years of experience as a CFO and investment advisor. He is a member of the Institute of Certified Financial Planners (ICFP), The Financial Planning Association (FPA), and The Investment Management Consultants Association (IMCA).

FIRM: A registered, fee-only, investment advisory firm that provides financial and investment management services to individuals, trusts, retirement plans and small- to medium-sized businesses. Activities are oriented toward comprehensive financial planning services, with emphasis in the areas of investments, retirement, and estate planning.

Brent E. Bentrim, CFM
Carolopolis Family Wealth Mgmt

TEL: 843.722.3232

EMAIL: brent.bentrim@carolopolis.net

LOCATION: Charleston, SC

BIO: Brent E. Bentrim is a Certified Estate Advisor and managing principal of his own investment advisory firm. He entered the industry in the mid-1990s with Merrill Lynch before joining a large private bank. Bentrim coaches his clients to envision their ideal future, develop a written strategic plan, and then implement smart financial and life strategies to achieve their goals and aspirations.

FIRM: Bentrim founded Carolopolis Family Wealth Management, LLC, an independent Registered Investment Advisor, in 2002. Its *"wealth of insight"* process is based on the belief that affluent investors demand and should expect to receive high-level advice and partnerships with their advisors.

Reginald A. T. Armstrong, RIA
Armstrong Wealth Mgmt Group

TEL: 843.292.9997

EMAIL: reginald.armstrong@lpl.com

LOCATION: Florence, SC

BIO: President and client wealth manager of Armstrong Wealth Management Group, Reginald A.T. Armstrong holds his Investment Advisor Representative license with Linsco/Private Ledger (LPL), member SIPC. He served as an officer in the United States Army and became a decorated combat veteran of Operation Desert Storm.

FIRM: Specializes in helping high-net-worth families, retirees and those about to retire, and corporate retirement plans grow and manage their wealth.

TEAM: Leslie D. Moore, client service manager; Claudine P. Yeager, service assistant; H. Lee Carter III, marketing director; and Jason W. Dorriety, marketing assistant

David J. Bromelkamp, CIMA
RBC Dain Rauscher

TEL: 612.371.2842

EMAIL: david.bromelkamp@rbcdain.com

LOCATION: Minneapolis, MN

BIO: David J. Bromelkamp is senior vice president with RBC Dain Rauscher where he leads a team of Certified Investment Management Consultants. He is a founding member of the Senior Consulting Group at RBC Dain Rauscher, which is an elite group of the firm's leading investment management consultants.

Bromelkamp is a member of the board of directors of the Minnesota Society of Certified Public Accountants and also serves as president of the Twin Cities Chapter of the Investment Management Consultants Association (IMCA). He speaks frequently on "best practices" of fiduciary investment management.

FIRM: Provides investment advisory services to institutional clients and accredited investors.

C-D

John Chiacchiero
Melhado, Flynn & Associates

TEL: 843.757.9339

EMAIL: jchiacchiero@melhadoflynn.net

LOCATION: Bluffton, SC

BIO: John Chiacchiero is an investment advisor with the Wealth Management Group of Melhado, Flynn & Associates, Inc. He received his BA in Finance from Mount Union College, and his MBA from Miami University. Prior to joining the company, Chiacchiero served six years as vice president/general manager of Lighthouse Investment Advisors and 10 years as a university lecturer in finance with the University of South Carolina, where he now serves as an adjunct lecturer, and at HOSTA College in Switzerland

TEAM: Michelle A. Myhre, CFP® (Certified Financial Planner); Christopher Kiesel, CFA, portfolio manager; Al Cerrati, investment advisor

Thomas Curran/Lisa T. Clifford
Curran Investment Management

TEL: 518.447.8492

EMAIL: tcurran@wachoviasec.com
lclifford@wachoviasec.com

LOCATION: Albany, NY

BIOS: Thomas Curran, MBA, is director of investments and Certified Portfolio Manager of Curran Investment Management of Wachovia. He has 30-plus years of industry experience and is dedicated to meeting the needs of individual and institutional investors.

Lisa T. Clifford is associate vice president. She develops client presentations and serves as liaison for the group's investment management and consulting services.

FIRM: Founded in 1996, Curran Investment Management of Wachovia is a results-oriented team of professionals dedicated to meeting clients' unique financial goals. Each member brings unique skills to the client relationships.

George Connell, Jr , CIMA
Washington Investment Advisors

TEL: 610.293.7201

EMAIL: gconnelljr@washingtoninv.com

LOCATION: Radnor, PA

BIO: George W. Connell Jr. has 20 years of experience as president and chief investment officer of Washington Investment Advisors. He is responsible for the creation, continued development and implementation of the firm's overall investment strategy. Connell earned the Certified Investment Management Analyst (CIMA) accreditation from the IMCA in conjunction with the Wharton School of The University of Pennsylvania. He holds Series 7, 63 and 65 NASD licenses.

FIRM: Washington Investment Advisors focuses on large-capitalization, high-quality, A-rated, companies – each an industry leader. This provides the basis for investment portfolios managed by the firm.

Frederick J. Dawson, ChFC, CLU
Bassett, Brosius & Dawson, Inc

TEL: 302.999.9330

EMAIL: fdawson@bbdinc.com

LOCATION: Wilmington, DE

BIO: With 22 years of comprehensive wealth management experience, Frederick J. Dawson is founding principal partner and vice president of Bassett, Brosius & Dawson, Inc. (1981). He has been published nationally and internationally and has made guest appearances on numerous radio and television programs. In 2003, he was named "Entrepreneur of the Year" by New Castle County Chamber of Commerce.

FIRM: Services a diverse domestic and international client base, including professionals, retirees, widows/widowers, professional musicians, and business owners.

TEAM: Terry Ann Heidt, executive assistant; Harriet Lang Chappell J.D., CFP, staff attorney; Brian D. Dawson, ChFC, CIMC, financial advisor

Donald C. DeWees Jr, CIMA, CIS
DeWees Investment Consulting Grp

TEL: 302.428.8614

EMAIL: ddewees@wachoviasec.com

LOCATION: Greenville, DE

BIO: Senior vice president–investments of DeWees Investment Consulting Group of Wachovia Securities, Donald C. DeWees Jr. joined his father's firm in 1993. In 1996, he achieved his CIMA designation and in 2001, his Investment Fiduciary Auditor (IFA) certification.

FIRM: Specializes in designing and implementing coherent investment strategies for high-end retail and small institutional clients and providing an incomparable level of service driven by their "referral only" practice.

TEAM: Principals include: Don DeWees Sr., Arta Vitoloa, CFP; relationship managers include: Cecelia Dugan, CFP; Tamara Bowers, Colleen Weaver, Cheri Breuer, Thomas Kenney Debbie Hinderhofer

Barbara B. Hudock
Hudock Moyer Financial Advisors

TEL: 570.326.9500

EMAIL: bhudock@attglobal.net

LOCATION: Williamsport, PA

BIO: Managing principal and member of the Investment Committee of HMFA, Barbara B. Hudock has 27 years of experience in the financial services industry. She is a CIMA candidate and holds her Series 7, 24, and life and health insurance licenses. Barbara was awarded the Dalbar Financial Professional Seal, awarded to financial professionals who have met the standards in client performance, trust and satisfaction.

TEAM: Partner– Jason J. Moyer (CFP®); staff members– Wayne Dieffenderfer, financial advisor; Deanna Gephart, registered service Manager; C. Jane Hawkins, client relations coordinator; Holy Tagliaferri, communications specialist; Michael Hudock, financial advisor

James M. Harris III, CFP®, CIMA
The Harris Group of Morgan Keegan

TEL: 229.432.8428

EMAIL: james.harris@morgankeegan.com

LOCATION: Albany, GA

BIO: After graduating from Georgia Southern University in 1990 with a bachelor's degree in banking/finance, James M. "Jay" Harris worked as an investment consultant for Interstate/Johnson Lane. He became one of the youngest branch managers in the company's history. In 1993, he joined IJL Wachovia, eventually serving as first vice president of investments. In 2001, Jay joined Morgan Keegan & Company, Inc. as a senior vice president.

FIRM: Provides customized plans to suit clients' situations—clients decides how much they want to be involved. Known for its structure and flexibility of process.

TEAM: Nanette Jordan Stuart, sales assistant

Jack Krapf, CIMA /Douglas Aldridge
Aldridge, Johnson & Krapf

TEL: 478.722.8015

EMAIL: jack.krapf@wachoviasec.com
doug.aldridge@washoviasec.com

LOCATION: Macon, GA

BIOS: Jack Krapf, senior vice president, has more than 18 years of industry experience. He specializes in investment management consulting, asset allocation strategies and investment manager selection.

Douglas Aldridge, managing director, has more than 25 years of industry experience. He served as president of Interstate Johnson Lane – Wachovia Bank's full-service brokerage division – until 2001.

FIRM: Aldridge, Johnson & Krapf of Wachovia Securities.

TEAM: Clifford L. Johnson, first vp; Norris Broyles Sr., senior vp; Gable S. Hulbert, fa; Caroline S. Maloney, sr. account administrator

O-R

Martim DeArante-Oliveira, ChFC, CLU
H &S Financial Advisors

TELE: 650.926.1408

EMAIL: moliveira@hoodstrong.com

LOCATION: Menlo Park, CA

BIO: Martim DeArantes-Oliveira is principal at H&S Financial Advisors. He works with high-net-worth families and not-for-profit organizations across two different continents. Originally from Portugal, he began his career in financial services at Union Bank of Switzerland, in London, where he worked for the investment and private banking divisions. At UBS, Martim used his legal and financial training to create risk management and alternative investment strategies for high-net-worth individuals and organizations.

FIRM: An affiliate of Hood & Strong, LLP, CPAs. H&S delivers expert, integrated and independent financial advice to individuals and organizations.

Matthew N. Potter, CFP®, CIMC
Raymond James Financial Services

TELE: 307.638.9332

EMAIL: matthew.potter@raymondjames.com

LOCATION: Cheyenne, WY

BIO: Matthew N. Potter, branch manager and registered principal with Raymond James Financial Services, Inc, has been in the investment business since 1987. He is chairman of the Wyoming State Retirement System Board of Trustees and serves on the Investment Legislative, Deferred Compensation and Ethics Committees for the board.

Potter is a board member of the Southeast Wyoming Estate Planning Council and the Cheyenne Symphony, and is actively involved with the Lance Armstrong Foundation's Peloton Project, an organization for cancer victims.

FIRM: Matthew N. Potter, CFP, of Raymond James Financial Services, Inc., provides financial planning and investment consulting services.

Donald R, Parker, CFA®, AVA
Gryphon Valuation Consultants

TELE: 702.870.8258

EMAIL: dparker@bizvals.com

LOCATION: Las Vegas, NV

BIO: Donald R. Parker has more than 20 years of experience in providing investment management services. Upon graduation from college, he launched his career in finance at a money management firm in Orlando, FL, where he spent several years as an equity analyst. Parker eventually co-founded his own money-management company where he added the responsibility for portfolio management to his analytical duties. In 2000, he was named by Nelson's as one of the "World's Top 20 Best Portfolio Managers." Parker holds the Chartered Financial Analyst® designation, demonstrating a thorough understanding of the analysis and application of financial knowledge across the core areas of the investment management process.

Ira G. Rapaport, CPA, CIMA, CFP®
RINET Company

TELE: 617.488.2729

EMAIL: igr@rinetco.com

LOCATION: Boston, MA

BIO: Ira G. Rapaport, vice president of RINET company, is a fee-only financial advisor who has offered comprehensive wealth management services to high-net-worth individuals and families for more than 15 years. He provides unbiased investment advice in creating, implementing, monitoring and reporting on customized investment strategies, and has broad experience in developing tax-efficient investment strategies, asset allocation modeling and alternative investments. Rapaport is a member of the TIAA-CREF Financial Advisory Board and has been quoted and published in trade publications. He has spoken at many industry events.

FIRM: The RINET Company, LLC, is a subsidiary of Boston Private Financial Holdings (NASDAQ:BPFH)

Jeffrey B. Thomas, CIMC, JD, CPA
Raymond James Financial Services

TELE: 972.960.7023

EMAIL: jeff.thomas@raymondjames.com

LOCATION: Dallas, TX

BIO: Jeffrey B. Thomas has 25 years of experience helping high-net-worth individuals, trust beneficiaries and trustees of ERISA plans, foundations, endowments and personal trusts with their investment, tax, estate planning and fiduciary concerns. After 10 years of practicing law (JD) with an emphasis on tax and estate planning, he joined Raymond James Financial Services. He is a member of the national board of directors for the Investment Management Consultants Association (IMCA) and currently serves as treasurer, and Ethics Committee board liaison. Thomas is a faculty member for the Southern Methodist University Department of Continuing Education, teaching two classes. He an active member of the American Association of Attorney-CPA's.

James Whiddon, CFP®, ChFC, CLU
JWA Associates

TELE: 972.661.3355

EMAIL: jwhiddon@jwafinancialgroup.com

LOCATION: Dallas, TX

BIO: James N. "Jim" Whiddon, president and CEO, JWA Financial Group, Inc, began his financial services career in Dallas in 1986. He graduated with a Bachelor of Science degree from Texas A&M University in 1983, and a Master of Science in Financial Services from The American College in 1998. Whiddon is a frequent speaker, financial author and hosts a weekly radio program. In 2002 and 2003 he was named one of Dallas' "Best Financial Planners" by *D Magazine*.

FIRM: JWA Financial Group, Inc., is a registered investment advisor and independent financial advisory firm that specializes in retirement transition. It was identified as a "Top Dog" wealth management firm by Bloomberg in 2003.

Adam Westphalen, CIMA, CFP®, CPTx
Vista Financial Strategies

TELE: 203.377.4448 x201

EMAIL: adamwestphalen@aol.com

LOCATION: Stratford, CT

BIO: CIO and co-founder of Vista Companies, Adam Westphalen is dedicated to assisting individuals, families and business owners in the areas of investment and retirement planning. He imparts invaluable knowledge of the capital markets, investor behavior and effective implementation methods. He is also a CSA.

Previously with Price Waterhouse, LLP, in New York City, Westphalen founded Vista Companies when he was drawn to the unique financial goals of his client base, and wanted to help clients accomplish their goals in an independent, objective environment without the restrictions that existed in large firms.

FIRM: Vista Financial Strategies is a subsidiary of Vista Companies, LLC.

Stephen Winks
Society of Senior Consultants

TELE: 804.643.1075

EMAIL: www.SRConsultant.com

LOCATION: Richmond, VA

BIO: Stephen Winks is co-founder of The Society of Senior Consultants and publisher of *Senior Consultant*, a publication which serves top-tiered senior consultants who advise 25% of all U.S. assets. He is the leading proponent of the "high-level, comprehensive advice business model" that is shifting the way financial services firms conduct business. Winks also co-founded of Portfolio Construction Technologies, which pioneered the first internet-based, comprehensive investment process technology tied to a virtual real-time balance sheet and income statement. Winks speaks regularly at industry conferences and regional meetings of major financial services firms.

Asset Management ● The process of managing the capital of an individual or a corporation. A four-step system usually is followed which includes creating an investment policy statement, asset allocation (and re-balancing when necessary) performance monitoring, and performance reporting. The process also includes strategies to optimize the risk as well as the reward in the investor's portfolio.

Asset Allocation ● An investment portfolio that divides assets among major asset categories, such as bonds, stocks, or cash. The purpose is to balance risk and create diversification.

Bear Market ● A market in which prices of a certain group of securities are falling or are expected to fall. Although figures can vary, a downturn of 15%-20% or more in multiple indexes (Dow or S&P 500) is considered a bear market.

Bond ● A bond is considered a debt investment—loaning money to an entity (company or government) that needs funds for a defined period of time at a specified interest rate. In exchange, the entity will issue a certificate, or bond, that states the interest rate to be paid and when loaned funds are to be returned (maturity date). Interest on bonds is usually paid every six months (semi-annually).

Bull Market ● A market in which prices of a certain group of securities are rising or are expected to rise.

Capital ● 1) Financial assets or the financial value of assets such as cash. 2) The factories, machinery, and equipment owned by a business.

CERTIFIED FINANCIAL PLANNER™ (CFP®) ● Certification marks awarded by the Certified Financial Planner Board of Standards, Inc. to individuals who successfully complete the CFP Board's initial and ongoing certification requirements. Those wanting to become a CFP professional must take extensive exams in the areas of financial planning, taxes, insurance, estate planning, retirement, among others. CFP professionals must also complete continuing education programs each year to maintain their certification status.

Certified Investment Management Analyst (CIMA) ● An advanced designation designed specifically for investment consultants, and offered through the Investment Management Consultants Association. To qualify, a designee must have three years of verifiable experience in the field of investment management consulting. This experience must reflect at least fifty percent of the advisor's time involves the consulting process.

Certified Investment Management Consultant (CIMC) ● Certifications awarded to financial professionals who have completed extensive course work and passed NASD proctored examinations for Levels I and II of the Institute for Certified Investment Management Consultants' (now IMCA) course. CIMCs must also meet IMCA's requirements concerning experience in consulting and managed accounts, and adhere to its code of ethics and continuing education requirements.

145

C-H

Chartered Financial Analyst™ (CFA®) ● A professional designation given by the Association for Investment Management and Research (AIMR) that measures the competence and integrity of financial analysts. Candidates are required to pass three levels of exams covering areas such as accounting, economics, ethics, money management, and security analysis.

Chartered Financial Consultant (ChFC) ● Designation awarded by American College of Bryn Mawr, PA, to a professional financial planner who completes a four-year program covering economics, insurance, taxation, real estate, and other areas related to finance and investing.

College for Financial Planning ● The oldest provider of financial planning education in the United States; delivers educational programs, courses, and materials. Also created the country's first financial planning education program—the CFP® Professional Education Program—as well as the CFP® designation.

Certified Public Accountant (CPA) ● Designation by the American Institute of Certified Public Accountants (ICPA) for those who pass an exam and meet work-experience requirements.

Commission ● A service charge assessed by a broker or advisor in return for buying and selling securities.

Diversification ● A risk management technique that mixes a wide variety of investments within a portfolio. It is designed to minimize the impact of any one asset class on overall portfolio performance.

Dow Jones Industrial Average ● The Dow Jones Industrial Average (DJIA) is a price-weighted average of 30 significant stocks traded on the New York Stock Exchange and the Nasdaq.

Due Diligence ● An investigation or audit of a potential investment or investment manager. Due diligence serves to confirm all material facts.

Equity ● 1) A term describing a stock, or any security, representing an ownership interest. 2) On the balance sheet, equity refers to the value of the funds contributed by the owners (the stockholders) plus the retained earnings (or losses). 3) In the context of margin trading, equity is the value of securities minus what has been borrowed from the brokerage.

Fiduciary ● A person legally appointed and authorized to hold assets in trust for another person, and manage those assets for the benefit of that person and not his/her own profits; this person is held personally liable.

Financial Planner ● An investment professional who assists individuals in putting together a financial plan and helps to coordinate various financial activities.

Hedge Fund ● An aggressively managed portfolio taking positions on safe and speculative opportunities. Most hedge funds are limited to a maximum of 100 investors. For the most part, hedge funds are unregulated because it is assumed the people investing in these are very sophisticated and wealthy.

IRA ● An Individual Retirement Account (IRA) is a retirement investing tool that can be either an Individual Retirement Account or an Individual Retirement Annuity. There are several types of IRAs: Traditional IRAs, Roth IRAs, SIMPLE IRAs, and SEP IRAs.

Inflation ● The rate at which the general level of prices for goods and services is rising, and subsequently, purchasing power is falling.

Inflation Risk ● The uncertainty over the future real value (after inflation) of your investment.

Institutional Investor ● A non-bank person or organization (insurance company, corporate pension plans, etc.) that trades securities in large enough share quantities or dollar amounts that they qualify for preferential treatment and lower commissions. Institutional investors face fewer protective regulations because it is assumed that they are more knowledgeable and better able to protect themselves.

Investment Advisor ● 1. A person making investment recommendations in return for a flat fee or percentage of assets managed, known as a commission. 2. For mutual fund companies, it is the individual who has the day-to-day responsibility of investing and monitoring the cash and securities within the fund's portfolio in accordance with the objectives.

Investment Policy Statement ● A written document describing financial goals, how capital will be invested, the target date for the accomplishment of the goals, and the amount of tolerable risk.

Large Cap ● Companies having a market capitalization between $10 billion and $200 billion.

Liability ● A legal debt or obligation estimated via accrual accounting

Life Insurance ● Income-protection in case the insured passes away. The named beneficiary receives the proceeds to offset that lost income.

Long Term ● Holding an asset for an extended period of time.

Managed Account ● An investment account that a professional money manager is hired to control.

Market Timing ● An attempt to sell a stock or portfolio when a market is at its high and buying at a low. Or, trying to leave the market entirely during downturns and reinvesting when it heads back up.

Market Value ● 1) The current quoted price at which investors buy or sell a share of common stock or a bond at a given time. 2) Sometimes referred to as total market

M-S

value, the market capitalization plus the market value of debt.

Modern Portfolio Theory ● A theory on how risk-averse investors can construct portfolios in order to optimize market risk against expected returns. The theory emphasizes that risk should not be viewed in a negative context, but rather as an inherent part of higher reward. According to the theory, an efficient frontier of optimal portfolios can be constructed offering the maximum possible expected return for a given level of risk.

Mutual Fund ● An investment product that gives small investors access to a well diversified portfolio of equities, bonds and other securities.

National Association of Securities Dealers(NASD) ● A self-regulatory organization of the securities industry responsible for the operation and regulation of the Nasdaq stock market and over-the-counter markets. It also administrate exams for investment professionals, such as the series 7 exam.

Net Worth ● The amount by which a person's assets exceed their liabilities.

Pension Plan ● A retirement plan, usually tax exempt, wherein the employer makes contributions for the employee. Many pension plans are being replaced by the 401K.

Portfolio ● A group of assets, such as stocks, bonds, and mutuals, that are held by an investor. To reduce their risk, investors tend to hold more than just a single stock or other asset.

Portfolio Manager ● The person responsible for the investment of a mutual fund's or separately managed account's assets, implementing its investment strategy, and managing the day-to-day portfolio trading.

Rating ● 1) An evaluation of a corporate or municipal bond's relative safety from an investment standpoint. It is the issuer's ability to repay principal and make interest payments. 2) An analyst's recommendation on whether to buy, sell, or hold a specific stock.

Registered Investment Advisor (RIA) ● Advisors who manages the investments of others and are registered with the Securities and Exchange Commission.

Risk ● The chance that an investment's actual return will be different than expected. This includes the possibility of losing some or all of the original investment. Usually measured using historical returns or average returns.

Risk Tolerance ● The degree of uncertainty an investor can handle in regards to a negative change in the value of their portfolio.

Securities and Exchange Commission (SEC) ● A government commission created by Congress to regulate the securities markets and protect investors. It also monitors corporate takeovers in the United States.

Sector ● A particular group of securities that are in the same industry.

S&P 500 ● Standard and Poors 500 Index; consists of 500 stocks chosen for market size, liquidity, and industry group representation. It is a market-value weighted index, with each stock's weight in the index proportionate to its market value.

Security ● An instrument representing ownership (stocks), a debt agreement (bonds), or the rights to ownership (derivatives).

Separately Managed Account (SMA) ● A private, individual investment account opened through a brokerage firm or an RIA in which the investor has direct ownership of the actual securities in the account. A SMA is managed by a professional money manager, and the investor can restrict the types of securities held in the account. A SMA also offers tax-efficiencies.

Separate Account Managers ● Trained professional money managers who manage an investor's private account.

Series 6 ● A securities license entitling holder to sell mutual funds and variable annuities.

Series 7 ● A securities license entitling holder to sell all types of securities products.

Small Cap ● Refers to stocks with a relatively small market capitalization. The definition of small-cap can vary but is generally a company between $300 million to $2 billion in market cap.

Stock ● Ownership in a corporation that is represented by shares. A holder of stock (a shareholder) has a claim on part of the corporation's assets and earnings.

Stockbroker ● 1) A professional who charges a fee or commission for executing buy and sell orders submitted by an investor.

Tax Efficient ● An investment that takes into account the effect any gains will have on taxable income.

Trend ● The general direction of the price of an asset or market in general

Trade ● A transaction involving the sale and purchase of a security.

Trend ● The general direction of the price of an asset or market in general.

Underperform ● An analyst recommendation that means a stock is expected to do slightly worse than the market return.

Value Added ● When a company or advisor enhances its product or service before offering it to its customers.

Wealth Management ● A professional service that can be the combination of financial/investment advice, accounting/tax services, and legal/estate planning for one fee.

Wire House ● A company with different branches that are linked by a communications system enabling the sharing of financial information, research, and prices; a national brokerage firm.